The History of Crime and Criminal Justice Series

David R. Johnson and Jeffrey S. Adler, Series Editors

T0158321

CONTROLLING
VICE

Regulating Brothel Prostitution in St. Paul, 1865–1883

JOEL BEST

Ohio State University Press • Columbus

© 1998 by The Ohio State University.
All rights reserved.

Library of Congress Cataloging-in-Publication Data

Best, Joel.
Controlling vice : regulating brothel prostitution in St. Paul,
1865–1883 / Joel Best.
p.   cm. — (History of crime and criminal justice series)
Includes bibliographical references and index.
ISBN 0-8142-0807-X (cl : alk. paper). —ISBN 0-8142-5007-6
(pa : alk. paper)
1. Prostitution—Minnesota—Saint Paul—History—19th century.
2. Sex oriented businesses—Law and legislation—Minnesota—Saint
Paul—History—19th century.   3. Prostitutes—Legal status, laws
etc.—Minnesota—History—19th century.   I. Title.   II. Series.
HQ146.S25B47   1998
306.74'09776'581—dc21
98-26486
CIP

Text and jacket design by Paula Newcomb.
Type set in Adobe Trump Mediæval by Nighthawk Design.
Printed by Bookcrafters, Inc.

The paper used in this publication meets the minimum requirements of the
American National Standard for Information Sciences—Permanence of Paper for
Printed Library Materials. ANSI Z39.48-1992
9 8 7 6 5 4 3 2 1

CONTENTS

PREFACE

In 1871, a group of respectable ladies risked their reputations to visit several brothels in Washington, D.C. They asked the establishments' madams about the realities of prostitution, its causes, and the prospects for reform. The ladies were "fully convinced that justice had never been done these women, and that the only way to ascertain their real condition, or to reclaim them, was to recognize them as sisters, women to be visited, to be conversed with, to be treated with consideration and respect."[1] This was not the last attempt to forge a bond of sisterhood between prostitutes and women reformers. A century after the Washington ladies' visits, the prominent feminist activist Kate Millett edited *The Prostitution Papers*, statements by two feminists and two prostitutes. Echoing the Washington ladies, Millett called for "a dramatic shift in perspective in the world of 'straight' women, historically divided from the prostitute by their respectability. There must be a new climate of awareness, of trust and self-respect between women, a feeling of community."[2]

A similar impulse helps explain the recent revival of scholarly interest in prostitution's history. Popularized histories of vice are an old, established genre—winking, romanticized narratives stringing together anecdotes emphasizing the brothels' elegance, the madams' refinement, and the prostitutes' beauty. Focusing on vice's naughty, titillating aspects, these accounts traditionally mixed fact, rumor, and outright fiction.[3] However, the new social history's emergence in the 1960s inspired a new generation of more professional historians. Calls to write "history from the bottom up," using census schedules, city directories, and other documentary evidence to reconstruct ordinary lives, led historians to study previously neglected sectors of society, including the working class, ethnic minorities, immigrants, and the underworld. In turn, in the 1970s, when public—and scholarly—attention began focusing on gender, feminist researchers relocated the history of prostitution, shifting it away from the history of crime or sexuality, redefining it as a part of women's history. A growing body of case studies that carefully mine local records now offers detailed—and very often feminist—analyses of prostitution in various cities.[4] Several recent titles invoke the familiar imagery of sisterhood: *Their Sisters' Keepers; Daughters of Joy, Sisters of Misery; The Lost Sisterhood*. These feminist analyses view prostitution as gendered criminality, a reflection of the limited choices available to women in a patriarchal society.

Studying gender requires examining men as well as women. The bedrock finding in criminological research is that crime tends to be committed by young males. Immigration—disproportionately young and male—ensured that males outnumbered females throughout the nineteenth century. Unable to afford marriage, many of these young men remained single, increasing their risks of becoming involved in crime and deviance. They formed the core of the nineteenth century's "bachelor subculture," a segment of the population prone to trouble, the core constituency of not just the jail but the saloon, the gambling hall, and the brothel. Thus, prostitution's history reflects both women's and men's history.[5]

Focusing on gender helps us address some—but not all—of the interesting issues raised by prostitution. For feminist activists and scholars, but also for legislators, police officers, and the general public, prostitution remains a knotty problem, symbolizing not only society's exploitation of women but also the more general threat of urban disorder. Prostitution raises issues of gender, but it also raises other issues, as evidenced in the tangled, contradictory history of reform campaigns to address the problem, to "do something" about prostitution.

Throughout American history, reformers have agreed on the need for new policies toward vice but disagreed about the nature of those policies. One reform tradition demands more aggressive policies aimed at eradicating and prohibiting prostitution. In colonial America, and in many cities during the early nineteenth century, angry mobs attacked brothels, destroying the buildings and forcing the women to flee. Later, ministers, respectable women, and other reformers began to speak out against prostitution, first in the late nineteenth century's social purity crusade, then as part of the Progressive movement. While condemning the prostitute, they typically viewed her as a victim, and concentrated their attacks on her exploiters—madams, pimps, white slavers, and the male customers who made vice possible. The movement to prohibit prostitution continues: during the 1970s, ministers sought to rescue teenaged girls who left the Midwest to become streetwalkers on New York City's "Minnesota Strip"; a decade later, the threat of AIDS led to new calls for eradicating prostitution.[6]

An opposing reform tradition seeks, not prohibition, but changes in the enforcement of antiprostitution laws. These reformers argue that laws against prostitution create more problems than they solve. Efforts to prohibit vice drive prostitution underground, where the lack of legal supervision fosters the spread of sexually transmitted diseases (now including AIDS), the involvement of pimps and organized criminals, and other social problems that arguably have consequences more serious than those of prostitution itself. These reformers believe that society would be better served if prostitutes operated openly, albeit under supervision. A landmark statement of this position was Dr. William Sanger's *The History of Prostitution*, published in 1858. As the administrator of New York City's venereal hospital, Sanger saw former prostitutes dying in misery; attempts at prohibition had not protected them, or the city's health. He urged that the government regulate vice, requiring regular medical inspections for prostitutes. During the late nineteenth century, reformers in various cities pressed for such regulation: the Washington ladies thought brothels should be licensed; in St. Louis, the 1870 Social Evil Ordinance required regular medical inspections; and New Orleans formally designated Storyville as its red-light district. These experiments were controversial. Advocates of prohibition attacked regulation as immoral, a compromise with evil. The Progressives' campaign for prohibition, coupled with demands, as

World War I approached, that soldiers and sailors be protected from disease and moral corruption, ended most local efforts to regulate vice. With the exception of Nevada, where prostitution is legally regulated in some counties, modern America is officially committed to a policy of prohibition.[7]

Still, some contemporary reformers continue to advocate regulatory policies. Modern feminists, like the Washington ladies before them, object to existing policies that punish women but not men. Although antiprostitution laws usually make it an offense to patronize a prostitute, customers are arrested and prosecuted far less often than prostitutes. This double standard of justice disadvantages women, even in periods when society's sexual attitudes are relatively liberal. In response, some feminists argue that prostitution should be decriminalized so that prostitutes at least have protection from discriminatory law enforcement. Organizations such as COYOTE (Call Off Your Old Tired Ethics), a prostitutes' guild, seek to unite feminists and prostitutes in social action to change the law, partially fulfilling the Washington ladies' dream of sisterhood.[8]

Concern over prostitution, then, appears repeatedly in American history, yet vice has remained an intractable social problem. Although respectable people ordinarily preferred to ignore it, prostitution never disappeared from American cities. Nor did it ever disappear as a focus for policy debates. For nearly two centuries, the police and other legal authorities have remained caught in the middle of the issue, trapped between reformers who demand that officials crack down and eradicate vice, and reformers who urge that some sort of regulation, rather than prohibition, should be the goal. Each side presents its own program as the only workable plan, and each points to fatal flaws in both the status quo and its opponents' proposals. The policy adopted in a given community—particularly in the nineteenth century—depended upon the relative influence of these competing factions; a city might experiment with regulation for a time, then give in to a moral crusade demanding prohibition, then return to largely ignoring prostitution, while still giving lip service to prohibition.

Although policies toward prostitution varied from one city to the next, reflecting local patterns of political influence, it is possible to speak of a national trend. During the second half of the nineteenth century, and into the first decades of the twentieth when the

Progressives' campaign for prohibition triumphed, many cities tried to regulate vice. Typically, this policy was neither formal nor overt; the authorities adopted a rhetoric of prohibition but, through their actions, sought to supervise and restrain, rather than eliminate, prostitution. This book offers a case study of one such city's experiment with regulation. From 1865 to 1883, officials in St. Paul, Minnesota, arrested and fined brothel madams at regular intervals. At first glance, these arrests might seem aimed at prohibition, but St. Paul's authorities expected that the brothels would remain open. They used arrests to bring the city income and, far more important, to give the police leverage to control the brothels, minimizing crime and other potential problems. St. Paul's policy was not unique; in cities across the country, officials adopted similar quasi-formal policies of regulation.

This book is both a historical and a sociological study. As a case study, it adds an important dimension to the history of prostitution in America. Historical research on prostitution has concentrated on a few cities with large, notorious vice districts or dramatic regulatory schemes: a good deal has been written about prostitution in New York, in San Francisco, and on the frontier, and about regulation in St. Louis and New Orleans. Far less is known about prostitution and its control in more typical American cities, cities without heavily imbalanced sex ratios and huge red-light districts, where regulation was covert. Studying St. Paul offers another perspective on the place of vice in late nineteenth-century middle America. In addition, numerous traces of St. Paul's system of regulation remain, making a richly detailed description of the city's brothels possible.

In addition to contributing to historical knowledge about prostitution, this book also examines an important issue in the sociology of deviance and social control. Sociologists of deviance usually take it for granted that prohibition is the goal of social control, largely ignoring regulation and other alternative social control strategies. By studying the regulation of St. Paul's brothels, we can begin to repair this oversight, developing a better understanding of different strategies of social control. While chapters 1 through 6 offer a case study of regulation in St. Paul, chapter 7 addresses the neglected topic of regulation as a social control strategy.

Acknowledgments

My greatest debt is to John Modell, a historian who knows a great deal about sociology, and who found it perfectly natural that a sociologist would want to learn some history. He introduced me to his discipline and guided me through the early stages of this project, commenting on innumerable early drafts. He continually encouraged me to expand my vision, to place what happened in St. Paul in its larger context.

I also owe thanks to those who helped me locate and gather source materials. Former St. Paul chief of police Richard H. Rowan and former deputy chief James S. Griffen gave me access to the manuscript arrest ledger. Staff members of the Minnesota Historical Society, the Wisconsin State Historical Society, and the Ramsey County Records Center helped me locate materials in their collections. I especially want to thank Ann Regan of the Minnesota Historical Society for answering some of my questions. Finally, Judy Young and Joan Best assisted me in collecting and organizing the data.

Several people commented on portions of the manuscript, giving me good advice (which I didn't always take). B. R. Burg, Barbara Sherman Heyl, Barbara J. Steinson, and, of course, John Modell all made valuable suggestions. David F. Luckenbill and Loy Bilderback deserve special mention; they read drafts of the entire manuscript and found many ways to improve it. At a later stage, Joel B. Grossman's critical reading and discussions with Andrew Altman helped me refine some key distinctions. I am grateful for all of this help.

A shorter version of chapter 3 appeared in the *Journal of Interdisciplinary History*; portions of chapter 2 and chapter 5 appeared, in very different forms, in *Minnesota History* and *Research on Social Policy*. A small grant from the California State University, Fresno Foundation helped support some of my early work on this project.

1

REGULATING DEVIANCE

Just after one o'clock on the morning of November 17, 1869, fire broke out in the two-story frame building at 18 West Eighth Street in St. Paul, Minnesota. The fire spread to the building next door, destroying both houses within two hours. The buildings' occupants, firefighters, and other spectators worked to save the furnishings and keep the fire from spreading further. More than most, this fire was news. When readers turned to the page of local news in that morning's *St. Paul Pioneer,* they found the headline: "A Big Fire! Mother Robinson's Establishment Destroyed." The afternoon *Dispatch* led with: "A Landmark Gone."[1]

The fire was newsworthy, not only because of its size but because the two houses belonged to Mary E. Robinson. Robinson was familiar to the newspapers' readers; she had appeared in dozens of news stories, often referred to respectfully as "Mrs. Robinson." She was a widow, "quite a ladylike appearing person," forty-three years old, with substantial local holdings.[2] When the census enumerator spoke with her the following spring, she would declare $2,000 in personal property and $75,000 in real property. She may well have been St. Paul's most successful female entrepreneur. She was a madam.

The buildings at 18 and 20 West Eighth Street were, respectively,

Robinson's brothel and her personal residence. The brothel was the city's largest, with seven prostitutes present on the night of the fire. Moreover, it was notorious as "the leading and, so to speak, the fashionable resort for men of easy virtue, and the abiding place of the more select among the 'soiled doves' of the city. . . . The reputation of the establishment was extended far and wide, and its existence was well known to every citizen of St. Paul."[3]

Covering the fire gave the newspapers a rich opportunity to titillate their readers with glimpses of brothel life. The initial *Dispatch* story noted, "Both houses were furnished in superb style"; Robinson's residence contained "a splendid library," while the brothel's furniture "was in black walnut sets."[4] But the controversy surrounding the fire's origin led to far more interesting revelations. Shortly before the fire began, George W. Crummey (proprietor of St. Paul's most notorious gambling hall), Thomas "Red-Handed Mike" Hanley (a local prizefighter), and P. O'Regan (a saloon keeper) had entered the brothel. A violent argument broke out between Crummey and Robinson. Robinson fled to her residence and, a few minutes later, the fire started. Robinson accused Crummey of setting the fire; he denied it. When the police declined to bring criminal charges of arson, Robinson sued Crummey and his companions in civil court for $28,000 in damages. The *Pioneer* and the *Press* gleefully printed Robinson's formal complaint, including detailed inventories of the items lost in the fire. And, in May 1870, all of the local papers reveled in the four-day trial, printing transcripts of the prostitutes' testimony, while lamenting that no gentlemen outside Crummey's party stepped forward to describe what they had seen. The case ended in a hung jury.[5]

Neither the fire nor the verdict could end Robinson's career as a madam. The buildings were insured. Always willing to talk to the press, she vowed on the day after the fire: "I shall take care of these girls, and at once put up *a splendid stone building for my business.* I have the money and own the ground and no one can prevent me from building. I will put up something that George Crummey or any other man can't burn down."[6] In 1874, after operating her brothel for over eight years and accumulating more than eighty arrests on charges of keeping a house of ill fame, Robinson announced her retirement and sold the brothel's contents at public auction.[7] "A woman of more than ordinary ability," she remained in the city, actively pursuing her real estate interests.[8]

The clamor surrounding the burning of Robinson's brothel is interesting because it contradicts the prevailing image of Victorian sexuality as suppressed and covert. Milton Rugoff argues that "the American Victorians were ostentatious in the outward observance of old taboos."[9] In this view, public life respected the demands of propriety, while prostitution, abortion, and other "vices" existed only in the shadows of the underworld. The reactions to the fire on Eighth Street revealed rather different attitudes. St. Paul's newspapers delighted in covering the fire and its aftermath. Their stories assumed that readers were familiar with and interested in Robinson and her business. They teased the respectable men who had visited the brothel that night, threatening to publish "the roll of honor." News coverage of the fire, as well as the printing of Robinson's inventory of lost property and the trial testimony, consumed multiple columns of space in four-page daily newspapers that rarely devoted more than two or three columns to local news. Moreover, none of the coverage expressed surprise at the established presence of brothels and gambling "hells" in St. Paul. Robinson was expected to reopen shop, although the *Dispatch* did hope she would move "the den to some more secluded spot."[10] And, of course, a suit by the city's leading madam, accusing its leading professional gambler of destroying the leading brothel, was treated seriously by the legal establishment. If Robinson's business was not respectable, neither was it hidden underground.

Robinson's status as a familiar public figure is not the mystery it might seem. Prostitution in post–Civil War St. Paul was not wide open, but neither was it hidden in the manner supposedly demanded by Victorian propriety. The men who set the city's public policy wanted prostitution kept under control. But they did not equate control with suppression; in fact, they assumed that efforts to eradicate vice would lead to its getting out of control. So, instead of trying to drive Robinson and her colleagues out of business, the authorities sought to supervise how the women did business. The officials used existing laws against prostitution as tools with which to regulate the brothels, seeking to keep the city's disorderly houses orderly.

"Business Is Business"

Very simply, St. Paul's city government took laws that prohibited prostitution and enforced them so as to make vice a quasi-legitimate business. Once each month, Mary E. Robinson and the city's other madams appeared in police court, where they were arrested, charged, convicted, and fined for keeping houses of ill fame. They were then free to leave the courtroom and return to their brothels, where they could conduct business without interference from the authorities until the next month's required courtroom appearance. In effect, each "trial" gave a madam a one-month license to manage a brothel; fining the women was not so much a punishment as a tax. The irony of using the criminal justice system to license crime was not lost on the public. One newspaper story describing a regular courtroom appearance by the madams read: "The City Treasury received yesterday from Dutch Henriette, Kate Hutton and Cora Webber the modest sum $162.40. Business is business."[11]

The practice of arresting and fining St. Paul's madams once a month is vulnerable to misinterpretation. At first glance, it might seem economically motivated: officials fined madams to generate revenue for the city. While the fines did bring the city some money, it seems unlikely this was a major consideration. The sum involved amounted to only a tiny fraction of the city's budget and, while officials were quite willing to defend the system of arrests and fines, their defenses never invoked economic arguments. A second misinterpretation would be to view the system as corrupt. The madams were not bribing the authorities. Again, while corruption tends to be secretive, the system operated openly. The money that changed hands went into the city's coffers, not individuals' pockets. The system had its critics, who attacked it on many grounds, but significantly, they never charged that corruption was involved. A third error is to view the arrests as an aberration, an instance when officials lost sight of what they wanted and how they ought to achieve it. St. Paul's officials were, in fact, quite conscious of what they were doing and why. They occasionally tinkered with the system, for instance, arresting madams only every other month, and twice they deliberately halted the arrests, only to begin again. The system existed because the city's officials believed it served important ends. And St. Paul was not alone; during the late nineteenth century, dozens of other cities had similar policies of arresting madams at regular intervals.

Not everyone approved of these policies. In St. Paul, influential people, including politicians, ministers, and well-to-do property holders, repeatedly attacked the system of monthly arrests. They charged that the madams' routine courtroom appearances distorted the legal apparatus. The laws against prostitution were intended to prohibit vice, but the system used those laws to ensure vice's perpetuation. Worse, the system placed the city in the immoral posture of not just tolerating brothels but, through the fines, sharing their profits. The critics mounted repeated reform campaigns to abolish the system. Yet the system continued to operate, not because it was a secret, or because there were no objections raised against it, but because the authorities believed, in spite of the criticism, that the policy of regular arrests was desirable.

What did St. Paul's officials gain from the policy? The officials argued that prostitution was inevitable, that no society in human history had successfully eradicated vice. Laws might prohibit vice, and vigorous enforcement might drive the women underground, but that would only make matters worse. Once underground, prostitution could not be supervised. There would be robberies and assaults. White slavery could flourish. Disease would spread. Prostitution itself might expand, migrating outward from the heavily policed vice districts with their saloons and gambling hells, into respectable residential neighborhoods, where the women might escape notice by the police. In short, cracking down on prostitution might crack the community's moral foundation. It was better to keep an eye on prostitution, to make sure that it didn't get out of control. By, in effect, licensing brothels, the authorities made the madams partners in keeping vice orderly. A madam who kept her house under control could operate without interference, but a woman who let things get out of hand would be driven out of business. The system of regular arrests ensured control; it regulated prostitution.

This system for regulating St. Paul's brothels resembles other arrangements for regulating vice. Many late nineteenth- and early twentieth-century cities sought to regulate prostitutes, but not all chose the method of regular arrests. Most cities adopted policies of geographic segregation, formally—or more often informally— restricting prostitutes to particular districts and leaving them alone so long as they stayed there. A few cities adopted more controversial programs, actually licensing prostitutes who passed regular medical inspections. These early efforts to regulate prostitution have counterparts in modern programs to control other vices. Every state has an alcohol control agency that licenses vendors and supervises when, where, to whom, and in what form alcoholic beverages may be sold. Similarly, legalized gambling involves systems of licensing and inspection for compliance with a wide range of regulations. And more regulatory policies may emerge in the future. Critics of drug laws call for the decriminalization of marijuana and other drugs; their proposals typically assume that drug use, while legal, would be regulated.

Given the fact that vice is often regulated, it is surprising how little sociological attention regulation receives. Sociologists of deviance and social control study vice and the societal reactions to it, but their basic assumptions often cause them to overlook regulation as a form of social control. These assumptions must be examined before St. Paul's regulated brothels can be placed in their larger context.

Deviance and Social Control Strategy

Deviance, as sociologists use the term, refers to acts that violate social norms, making the offender subject to sanctions.[12] The norms must be of some importance: murder is clearly deviant, but most sociologists would not include minor rule violations, such as improper table manners, in the category. Deviance cannot be understood without also understanding the nature of social control. If a society has rule breaking (deviance), it must also have rule making and rule enforcing (social control). Deviance and social control are inevitably intertwined. Yet, while there are many books about the nature of deviance, much less has been written about the social control of deviance.

While classical sociology defined social control very broadly as any group's capacity to regulate itself, contemporary sociologists of deviance usually adopt a narrower focus. Most analysts study deviance in the contemporary United States or western Europe, and they tend to portray social control in terms of official social control agents, such as police officers, judges, and psychiatrists, authorized to identify and sanction deviants in those societies. Thus sociologists of deviance, at least implicitly, define social control narrowly, as an official apparatus for sanctioning deviants.[13] Typically, these analysts assume that social control agents share a standard set of beliefs, resources, and tactics. But this is too simple. A more accurate analysis must begin by examining the interplay of deviants and agents in rule enforcement.

Once a rule exists, it must be enforced. Deviant acts are liable to sanctioning. This does not mean that every deviant act will be sanctioned; obviously, many deviants get away with many of their offenses. But every deviant must take the risk of being sanctioned into account. The fact that an act is deviant, that those who commit it are subject to sanctions, separates deviance from respectable activities. Deviance demands secrecy and other precautions. Deviants may try to keep the very fact of their deviant acts secret (as when addicts use drugs in private), or they may try to keep from being identified as offenders (as when robbers wear masks); even deviants who avow responsibility for their offenses (such as political terrorists) try to avoid apprehension. The need to ward off rule enforcers and their sanctions forms a central theme in the deviant experience.

In turn, the social control agents charged with rule enforcement must cope with the deviants' attempts to evade sanctioning. Agents may adopt various tactics to help them penetrate the deviants' secrecy. For example, undercover investigators disguised as drug users can witness illicit drug sales in private places. As deviants become familiar with the social control agents' tactics, they devise new defenses. The resulting process is one of escalation, with deviants increasing their efforts to ward off sanctioning and social control agents trying new ways of bringing sanctions to bear. The evolution from the very modest social control apparatus of the early nineteenth century to modern social control agencies with their extensive array of technologically and organizationally sophisticated tactics reveals this escalation.[14] At any stage in this process, the relative advantage may rest with either the agents or the deviants, but social control agents' efforts to enforce rules always impinge upon deviants to some degree, forcing them to consider the risk of sanctions.

Of course, social control does not affect all deviants to the same degree. Some deviants are relatively invulnerable to control efforts. In particular, those engaged in deviant exchanges are less vulnerable than those who exploit unwilling victims. In rape, robbery, and other forms of deviant exploitation, the victim is likely to ask social control agents for help, bringing the case to official attention. In contrast, deviant exchanges involve an individual supplying a forbidden good or an illicit service to another. Deviant exchange only requires that there is a demand for illicit goods or services, that someone is willing to supply them, and that customers and suppliers locate one another in an illicit marketplace. The actors have compatible interests; each voluntarily enters the exchange relationship, expecting to benefit from it. Because the participants in a deviant exchange are willing, neither believing that he or she is the target of exploitation, these transactions pose serious challenges for social control agents. In a deviant exchange, the participants share an interest in secrecy, in being discreet and avoiding the agents' attention. Neither participant is likely to report the illicit transaction. As a consequence, agents must first uncover deviant exchanges before they can sanction the participants.[15]

In addition to finding some forms of deviance more difficult to control, social control agents also vary in their ideologies, resources, and priorities, and these differences affect the agents' impact on deviants. Social control ideologies are systems of ideas for understanding deviance and justifying action against it. Currently, American social control agents have two principal, rival ideologies: the legal model, adopted by the criminal justice system, holds offenders responsible for their crimes and subjects them to punishment; while the medical model, advocated by the mental health system, argues that deviants are sick and in need of treatment. (There are other possible bases for social control ideologies—political models of disloyalty, religious models of sin, and so on.) The choice of a social control ideology is consequential; ideology shapes the agents' perception of both deviance and suitable social control tactics.[16]

Social control resources include the number of social control agents, their level of experience, and limits on their authority, as well as information, equipment, and facilities for handling deviants. The greater these resources, the more likely deviants will be sanctioned. But most agents' resources are limited; they cannot sanction all offenders. As a consequence, agents must set priorities, designating some offenses as more important than others and concentrating their resources on high-priority deviance. Agents often derive their priorities from their ideology, but they are also responsive to political pressure. Powerful people within a society may demand that agents pay more attention to particular offenses, or a moral crusade—a social movement against deviance—may cause agents to shift their priorities. As agents' resources and priorities fluctuate, so does the deviant's risk of being sanctioned.[17] For instance, police are more likely to make drug arrests if parents complain that their children are being exposed to drugs and demand action, or if the city government funds a special antidrug squad. Social control ideology, resources, and priorities shape the environment within which both agents and deviants must operate.

Social control agents also adopt varying strategies. This is a neglected topic. While carefully analyzing differences in agents' ideologies, resources, and priorities, sociologists have paid less attention to strategies of social control. Discussions of the topic tend to be circumscribed, defining strategies very narrowly, really at the level of tactics, rather than that of strategies. Thus, a researcher may note that undercover drug investigations are designed to increase drug arrests and disrupt the illicit drug traffic. Or a more sophisticated examination of the same program may reveal goal displacement, where organizational concerns, such as gaining more funding or promotions for members of the antidrug unit, may emerge as goals in their own right.[18] But both approaches focus on narrow tactical issues, looking at specific methods of particular social control programs. Neither considers broader issues of strategy—the overall plan of action for achieving general social control goals. Such broader, strategic questions include: Why are drugs viewed as deviant? and What should social control agents try to do about drugs?

Most sociological analyses of social control neglect overall strategy by concentrating on specific tactics. The agents' strategic approach is taken for granted by analysts—and by the agents themselves. This is not surprising. Social control agents operate within a well-defined organizational environment. As organizational members, they worry about short-term issues—the status of their current cases, the backlog of unfinished cases, their need for additional resources, or the possibility of adopting new, more effective tactics. They are less likely to raise strategic questions that might place the organization's purpose and worth in doubt. Similarly, sociologists who study social control agents come to focus on the agents' concerns and find it easy to build analyses around those issues.[19] Except for the rare cases when someone—usually an outsider—calls the agents' strategic purpose into question, as in reformers' arguments that antimarijuana laws are misguided and should be abolished, neither agents nor sociologists have reason to become especially interested in social control strategy.[20]

As a consequence, sociologists' references to social control strategy tend to make unexamined assumptions. Most important, they assume that social control agents are dedicated to the prohibition of deviance. Here, as elsewhere in the literature about deviance, the criminal justice system serves as an implicit model: the apparatus of police, courts, prisons, and related agencies seems designed to prohibit crime by punishing criminals; certainly the rhetoric of crime control promotes prohibition as the goal. But no one seriously expects to successfully prohibit crime. Crime will never totally disappear, if only because the criminal justice system cannot be totally responsive: some criminals are not deterred by the threat of punishment; some crimes go unnoticed; and other offenses go unpunished. Because the strategy of prohibition can never be completely successful, agents and analysts prefer to evaluate the effectiveness of control agents' tactics, with their modest, attainable goals. So, once more, attention drifts away from strategy toward tactics.

By uncritically assuming that social control agents always adopt a strategy of prohibition, sociologists can fail to understand the actual workings of social control. Frequently, forcing the agents' actions into the framework of prohibition distorts the agents' intent and makes it harder to evaluate their efficacy. In particular, agents may adopt a strategy of regulation—choosing to let deviance continue within certain limits. When viewed in terms of a policy of prohibition, the agents' regulatory work may seem ineffective, even though they are accomplishing more or less what they set out to do. The failure to critically examine the assumption that agents intend to prohibit deviance interferes with analysis. In contrast, this book seeks to hold the focus on social control strategy. The standard, albeit unstated, assumption that social control agents always adopt a strategy of prohibition needs to be challenged.

Plan of the Book

Most of this book is a case study of social control using a strategy other than prohibition—regulation. It examines the control of brothel prostitution in St. Paul, Minnesota, from 1865 to 1883. During these years, brothels held a quasi-legitimate status in St. Paul. Technically, throughout this period, prostitution violated both state law and city ordinance; prostitutes could be punished by substantial fines or a year's imprisonment. But St. Paul's police enforced these laws selectively, aiming to regulate, rather than prohibit, vice. Once each month, the city's madams appeared before the police court and were assessed modest fines. Under this system, madams who paid their fines and otherwise cooperated with the authorities did not risk more severe sentences. The system was openly acknowledged by city officials, who justified it as a realistic response to the practical problems of controlling vice.

The fact that St. Paul openly regulated its brothels makes the city's prostitutes and social control system unusually accessible to historical analysis. St. Paul's officials carefully kept track of the madams' courtroom appearances. The court dockets and other official records, including a register of prostitutes kept by the police, survive. Moreover, the city's newspapers did not treat vice with Victorian modesty; they printed hundreds of stories about prostitution. The city government's announced policy of regulation freed the press from the restraints of conventional propriety. There was no need to pretend shock that St. Paul had prostitutes. Further, the city's madams had no reason to hide. They spoke to reporters, gave their occupation to census takers, and appeared in other standard sources, such as city directories. Deviance is often largely hidden from historians, but, during these years, St. Paul's brothels remain remarkably visible.

This visibility permits a close examination of regulation's workings. Several facets of this neglected strategy deserve attention. First, it is important to ask how the policy works. How do social control agents attempt to regulate deviance? Which aspects of deviance do the agents work to control? What are the practical consequences of the policy for the agents who administer it? Second, the policy's impact on the illicit marketplace for vice deserves attention. What are the consequences for the market's suppliers, the deviants? What are the consequences for customers, and for others who also have ties to the marketplace? Third, what is the place of regulation in the larger community? How does regulation impinge on the community's various political, economic, and status interests? To what degree are the different elements in the community aware of and concerned about the policy? What are the objections to regulation, and who voices then? Who defends the policy? How are policy debates resolved?

The remaining chapters explore St. Paul's system of regulation and its consequences in an effort to answer these questions. Chapter 2 begins by trying to place St. Paul's system within its national context. During the second half of the nineteenth century, Americans began paying increasing attention to prostitution. Medical authorities argued that prostitutes were the principal vector in the spread of venereal disease; reformers charged that the women were victims of the male-dominated, anonymous city; and ordinary citizens objected to the presence of vice near their homes. In response, various prostitution control programs emerged on both national and local levels. They differed in their methods and goals, but all sought to cope with the problems posed by prostitution. St. Paul's system of regulating brothels through regular arrests was one such program. It was intended to control specific practical problems associated with vice and, in most respects, it did what it was supposed to do.

The next two chapters examine regulation's consequences for the women who worked within the system. Chapter 3 focuses on the careers of those who passed through St. Paul's brothels as madams or prostitutes. Nineteenth-century sexual ideology argued that a woman, once fallen, was ruined, permanently condemned to deviance. Moralists' descriptions of prostitutes' lives emphasized that isolation, poverty, disease, and death inevitably awaited. The evidence left behind by St. Paul's prostitutes reveals a more complex picture. Some of these women lived short, brutal lives, but others did not. The women took many different pathways into, through, and back out of vice.

Chapter 4 demonstrates that brothels involved a complex web of relationships, linking madams, brothel inmates, pimps, customers, police officers, and other members of the urban community. During the nineteenth century, the contributions of these different actors to vice were not always well understood. Some reformers simplistically insisted, for example, that madams viciously exploited their inmates. Again, studying St. Paul's brothels exposes more complexity—a pattern of multifaceted relationships within the demimonde. Because St. Paul openly regulated vice, producing a wealth of records, a great deal can be learned about the lives of the women in its brothels. Of course, the contours of those lives were in part shaped by the regulatory policy's effect on the illicit marketplace.

Chapter 5 shifts the focus from the deviants to the city's respectable citizens. Nationally, critics attacked regulation on moral, political, and economic grounds. Locally, reformers mobilized several moral crusades against St. Paul's system, demanding that the authorities eradicate vice. These campaigns were not successful, largely because St. Paul's respectable population was not united against regulation. City officials, the press, and even the general public recognized some of the complexities of controlling deviant exchange. They saw regulation's flaws, but they also understood the limits of prohibition. The city's policy toward prostitution was repeatedly debated in public, as respectable people sought to define their goals for controlling vice and to design policies that could meet those goals.

Chapter 6 examines the aftermath of the nineteenth-century experiments with regulating prostitution in St. Paul and other cities. Concern about vice peaked in the Progressive Era when cities across the country abandoned their systems of regulation, officially adopting prohibition as a strategy. This shift in policy had some unanticipated consequences, such as increasing the vulnerability of some prostitutes to pimps and organized crime. St. Paul's experience suggests that social control agents can manage deviance through regulation—if they define their goals narrowly and accept the policy's costs. But this case study also shows the difficulty of establishing a policy that satisfies all segments of the respectable community; debates over illicit marketplaces do not have simple solutions.

Finally, chapter 7 attempts to locate the case study within the larger framework of the sociology of deviance and social control. Regulation can be contrasted with two other social control strategies—prohibition and prevention. Each strategy involves characteristic tactics and each has important limitations. As in St. Paul, agents often adopt a strategy of regulation to control illicit marketplaces. However, even after adoption, regulatory policies tend to remain vulnerable to attack, particularly from those grounding their arguments in moral principles. Debates over regulation reveal the interplay between politics and morality in setting social control policy.

2

CONTROLLING BROTHELS
IN ST. PAUL

Our widespread fascination with deviants lends itself to mythmaking. In the case of late-nineteenth-century brothels, a rich variety of images is available. Contemporary popular culture looks back on prostitution with fondness: Western movies and novels portray opulent frontier bagnios, populated by shrewd madams and whores with hearts of gold. Popular histories of vice and fictionalized autobiographies of madams describe prostitution as a naughty episode in the nation's youth, when the men were lusty and the hookers happy. These accounts feature amusing stock tales: the boy who is introduced to sex in the brothel; the prostitute who falls in love and marries a wealthy customer; the madam whose friends, including ranking police officers and wealthy businessmen, help her outwit outraged reformers; and so on. If vice is viewed through a rosy lens, the women become more beautiful, the brothel furnishings more tasteful, and the customers' conduct more refined with every retelling. Twentieth-century mythmakers have romanticized the Victorian brothel almost beyond recognition.

Myths about deviance serve a purpose. They remind us about the nature of transgression and its consequences. Although we may romanticize deviance at a distance, most myths remind us that

14

crime doesn't pay, that offenders get their just desserts. These themes were central to nineteenth-century images of prostitution. Vice occupied a prominent place in nineteenth-century social thought, as indicated by the popular euphemism for prostitution: it was "*the* social evil." The nineteenth century had its own myths about vice, but they were far grimmer than their modern counterparts. Most nineteenth-century authorities would have been astounded to know that the brothels of their period would be romanticized by future generations. However, while these writers agreed that prostitution posed a danger to society, they could not agree on the nature of the threat or the appropriate response.

The leading nineteenth-century American authority on vice was Dr. William W. Sanger, physician and administrator of New York City's venereal hospital. In 1858, he published *The History of Prostitution*, an influential book that went through several printings. Sanger traced prostitution through the ages, documenting the failure of policies of prohibition: "The lash, the dungeon, the rack, and the stake have each been tried, and all have proved equally powerless to accomplish the object. . . . admitting that all attempts to compel prostitutes to be virtuous have notoriously failed; has not the time arrived for a change of policy?"[1] Sanger insisted that a new approach was necessary because existing policies endangered the public health. He argued that prostitutes were the principal vector in spreading venereal disease—an epidemic that first infected customers, then later their innocent wives and, eventually, their children. History proved that prohibiting vice was impossible; the danger of syphilis—for which there was then no effective cure—demanded that something be done. Sanger therefore proposed regulation, placing New York's prostitutes under the supervision of a medical bureau within the police department. Regular inspections would detect infected women, who then could be removed from the illicit marketplace. Sanger's analysis and his proposed solution met with wide approval from other physicians; in many cities, doctors called for regulation of prostitution as a solution to the problem of venereal disease.

In most of these cities, the physicians faced opposition from another group of professional men with a very different image of vice. Clergymen led campaigns against regulation, often with the support of women reformers. These crusaders focused on the depravity of vice. Prostitution was immoral; it was a sin. Even the threat of venereal disease could not make tolerating prostitution acceptable. Rather, the problem's solution lay in prohibition: the police should work to eliminate prostitution, while community members should stop having sexual relations outside of marriage. Stricter law enforcement and increased morality would solve the problem of venereal disease. Further, these reformers noted that regulatory schemes incorporated a double standard; prostitutes would be inspected for disease, but their customers would not. Women could be forcibly hospitalized, but the laws proposed no parallel punishment for infected men. The English reform movement, led by Josephine Butler, campaigned against these inequities in that country's Contagious Diseases Acts, attacking any plan that would invade the privacy of potentially respectable women (through a physical examination). In their attacks on vice, reformers often emphasized the essential innocence of women, even those who entered prostitution. Many prostitutes were seduced and then abandoned by lovers; others were tricked or forced to enter brothels. Thus, in addition to being sinful itself, prostitution depended upon immoral, criminal activities for its supply of women. Regulation tolerated seducers, white slavers, and pimps. For the clergymen and their women allies, the issues were clearly drawn. Morality and decency demanded that prohibition be the goal; regulation compromised with immorality.[2]

While physicians and clergymen debated public policy toward vice, most ordinary citizens remained silent. Some, of course, benefited from prostitution's presence; they were customers or had money invested in vice. A house rented to a madam, for example, brought its landlord far more than a respectable family could afford to pay. Other businesses, such as saloons, theaters, and night restaurants, also profited from the proximity of vice. On the other hand, many respectable citizens viewed prostitution as a blight on their communities. They worried that their sons and daughters might be corrupted. If prostitution could not be eradicated, these respectable citizens at least wanted it segregated. They complained about prostitutes parading in public places, wearing gaudy, expensive clothing and jewelry. Even more offensive were the public scenes of drunkenness and solicitation on the streets of the vice districts; respectable citizens who had to pass through vice districts to go about their business were outraged. For other citizens, the key issue was not prostitution's visibility but its threat to property values. Because brothels could pay landlords high rents, there was a constant danger of vice invading respectable neighborhoods. When a brothel moved into a neighborhood, respectable families fled, nearby properties could only be rented to vice interests, and a new vice district would be born. Many landlords, homeowners, and renters wanted to preserve their neighborhoods' respectability; they sought to protect their turf from invasion. Ordinary citizens might tolerate a vice district somewhere in their city, but they were not willing to have it nearby. They wanted prostitutes to be invisible and vice restricted to slums and other disreputable neighborhoods.[3]

Although physicians, clergymen, and ordinary citizens agreed that prostitution was an important social problem, they perceived the threat it posed to respectable society in very different ways. Physicians emphasized the threat to public health and clergymen focused on the threat of immorality, while ordinary citizens worried about vice directly infringing on their lives and homes. If these views were not inherently contradictory, at least they often came into conflict. Policy proposals by physicians to require medical inspections for prostitutes, like demands by citizens that vice be segregated in particular areas, often faced opposition from clergymen denouncing the toleration of sin. In St. Louis, physicians led a successful campaign to enact the 1870 Social Evil Ordinance—a plan requiring medical inspections—but clergymen rallied the opposition and ended the program after only four years. At that, the St. Louis experiment marked the physicians' greatest success. Although authorities in many cities expressed interest in the St. Louis program, moralists blocked virtually every attempt to regulate vice for medical purposes. Similarly, New Orleans developed the most notorious formal program for segregating vice. The city had a long and bitter history of brothels spreading into respectable neighborhoods. An 1898 ordinance effectively established the Storyville vice district by forbidding prostitution outside that area. Because the ordinance did not state that vice was legal within Storyville (that would have been contrary to state law), moralists had difficulty attacking the plan; the controversial ordinance remained in effect until 1917. But New Orleans was an exception. Most cities did not formally designate their vice districts for fear of being charged with tolerating immorality. For moralists, prohibition was the only acceptable policy.

The different perspectives of the physicians, clergymen, and ordinary citizens who concerned themselves with prostitution made it nearly impossible for any respectable community to formally, openly establish a social control policy of regulation.[4]

Leaders of the respectable community might debate the best policy toward vice, but they agreed that the police should play the key role in controlling prostitution. Police power lay behind plans for medical inspections; clergymen demanded more aggressive police work as the means of prohibiting vice; and ordinary citizens complained to the police about visible prostitution or the spread of brothels into respectable neighborhoods. But the police were more than the passive pawns of respectable interests. Like physicians and clergymen, the police had their own perspective toward prostitution. Vice posed particular problems for the police and the demands of police work shaped the officers' response to prostitution.

Sociological studies of modern police argue that the nature of police work shapes police activity. Police are charged with enforcing the law, but law enforcement is not a simple, straightforward task. Officers have considerable discretion, sometimes choosing to ignore clear violations, sometimes making unwarranted arrests. The use of discretion reflects the fact that law enforcement is not the only—or even the most important—police responsibility. Police also are expected to maintain order, to keep the peace. Peacekeeping is an ambiguous task; what is orderly varies from time to time, from place to place, and according to the beholder. Police must convert this ambiguity into activity; in doing so, they can use their legal powers to keep the peace. For example, officers may view certain types of people, such as drunks, juveniles, and prostitutes, as actual or potential sources of disorder, and, to maintain order, the police may deal with these troublesome people using various means, including persuasion, physical force, and the power to arrest. The officers' definitions of what constitutes potential trouble and what are appropriate responses are shaped not only by the law but by formal and informal department policies and such situational conditions as time of day, location, the presence or absence of bystanders, and so on. No legal code can adequately summarize what the police do. Ambiguities inherent in police work, such as situational definitions of order, shape the officers' responses.[5]

Like their modern counterparts, nineteenth-century police understood the realities of police work. Law enforcement was only part of their responsibility; they also were expected to maintain order. In particular, the nature of police work shaped their approach toward vice. Prostitution was not merely against the law. Urban brothels were often scenes of drunkenness, violence, and theft—incidents that demanded police attention. Prostitution was frequently less troublesome than the disorders it spawned. Moreover, most police officials acknowledged that prostitution, like drunkenness, could not be eradicated through law enforcement. Like physicians, nineteenth-century police officials were fond of pointing to prostitution's long history as proof that vice could not be suppressed. The marketplace for prostitution—formed by the demand for sexual services and the supply of women who could not find well-paying respectable work—was inevitable. Certainly, the police lacked the resources needed to prohibit vice, and the rest of the criminal justice system was no more efficient. Juries, for example, were reluctant to send madams to prison. But, if the laws could not be enforced, at least order could be kept, and most police departments sought a vice policy that would help keep their cities orderly.

The particular policy chosen by a city's police depended upon local expectations regarding vice and order. Some communities were more tolerant of prostitution than others. For example, where men greatly outnumbered women, as in western cattle towns, mining camps, and military bases, and also in some larger, more established cities, such as Oakland, the authorities ignored vice, except for flagrant offenses or on those occasions when citizens complained about a specific nuisance. Other cities sought to control vice through policies of geographic segregation: prostitutes would be tolerated within specified districts; found elsewhere, they would be arrested and punished. Most large cities, especially major ports, such as New York, New Orleans, and San Francisco, had large, sometimes quasi-official vice districts to meet the demands of a transient male population. Salt Lake City went so far as to wall off an area, permitting prostitutes to work within, but not outside, "the Stockade."[6]

Most historical case studies of prostitution focus on such communities: large, wide-open vice districts attract the researcher's attention. Less is known about prostitution in relatively stable communities where police were under more pressure to control vice.

Police standards also might vary within a given city. Behavior that was tolerated within the city's vice district might lead to arrest in a respectable neighborhood. Or the police might distinguish among types of prostitutes, adopting different standards for streetwalkers and brothels. Finally, a city's policies often changed over time. As communities grew and became more decorous, police responded to new orders from the city's government or demands by moralists or respectable citizens for a more orderly community.

The differences among these policies should not obscure the central characteristic they shared: virtually all nineteenth-century officials used a rhetoric of prohibition, yet many adopted policies that, in practice, tolerated prostitution's continued existence. Whatever the local boundary between acceptable and unacceptable conduct, order and disorder, the police were judged on their ability to keep vice within its borders, and their success was measured by the absence of complaints. When a mother sought the police chief's aid in rescuing her daughter from a "life of shame," or a group of homeowners demanded that the mayor do something about the new brothel in their neighborhood, the police were expected to act. Of course, complaints did not always result in action; when antiprostitution reformers denounced the continued presence of vice in the city, police officials might point to the imperfectability of humanity, the limited resources available to police, the reluctance of citizens to swear out complaints, and so forth. The police were responsible for the control of vice, but they usually defined their task as one of order maintenance. They were not trying to uphold morality or protect public health; they were keeping vice within its local, taken-for-granted place in the urban community. Because the police were responsible for defining and carrying out the local policy toward vice, each city's policy reflected police concerns with maintaining order. St. Paul is a case in point.

Vice and Order in St. Paul

During the twenty years following the Civil War, St. Paul grew rapidly. The population doubled during the 1860s (from 10,401 in 1860 to 20,030 in 1870), then redoubled during the next decade (to 41,473 in 1880). St. Paul was the state capital, a commercial center for people in Minnesota's smaller communities and a way station for settlers moving to the Northwest. As a river town, St. Paul served a substantial transient population. During the 1870s, it had a regional reputation for toughness and being a center of vice:

> Second, then Bench St., was most popular with such masses as daily sifted into the city; low river dives and dance halls, and groggeries, flourishing there, and no respectable man, much less a woman, dared enter the neighborhood after dark. Not a house on the Second Ward front but had its record of crime and vice; in one the gang of sharpers lying in wait for the approach of a "tenderfoot," in the other the relay of frail and tawdry women, ready to murder the souls of man, and in yet another the vender of distilled poison, destined to kill its victims, old men, young men, fair young girls and hideous hags—as fast as they could be led to slaughter.[7]

Official statistics supported this rowdy reputation. St. Paul's police reported in 1880 that the city had 7 brothels and 242 saloons, while Minneapolis, which had 5,000 more residents, claimed only 4 houses of prostitution and 176 saloons.[8]

The responsibility for keeping St. Paul orderly lay with its police force, an agency with modest resources. The department was small, numbering only 17 men in 1869 and 34 men twelve years later, roughly one officer for every 1,200 residents. There was considerable turnover; at least 55 men served in the department between 1869 and 1874, but only 6 remained on the roster throughout that period. In part, this reflected the practice of hiring an extra man or two to work during the busy summer months, but politics also played a major role in police appointments. City officers served one-year terms and, when the mayor's office changed hands—especially when the incoming mayor belonged to a different political party than his predecessor—the new administration often rewarded its supporters with positions on the force. Patrolmen covered their beats—some nearly a mile long—on foot. Because there was no patrol wagon for carrying prisoners, an arresting officer had to walk his prisoner to the jail. The *Pioneer* noted, "When a policeman in lower town makes an arrest he must leave his beat for nearly two hours to conduct his prisoner to the Hall. This is a very dangerous course at night especially."[9] Uncooperative prisoners posed serious problems for the officers, who often resorted to "rough and tumble methods" to bring them to jail.[10]

The city's inadequate jail facilities were the target of frequent police complaints. In 1875, Chief of Police James King described the wooden lockup's "dilapidated" condition: "The cells are insecure. I would suggest that at least two of the cells be made of iron. Often a half dozen of the most desperate characters are confined here, and under the circumstances the very strictest watch is necessary to prevent their escape."[11] Until 1879, the jail lacked separate cells for female prisoners; women were held at the Home of the Good Shepherd, a local refuge established in 1868 by Catholic nuns. The Magdalen Home, founded in 1873, also offered refuge to fallen women.[12]

Prostitution in St. Paul was not limited to the city's brothels. Some prostitutes claimed they were legitimately employed, often in the needle trades. In the 1880 census, the two young women living with George and Sarah Kimball—a notorious couple with a long history of arrests for managing brothels—listed themselves as dressmakers. This alibi was common enough that the city's leading newspaper sometimes used "plain sewing" as a joking euphemism for prostitution. Independent prostitutes—streetwalkers and others who worked outside brothels—were sometimes called "roomers" or "sewing girls."[13] Cigar stores, another common cover, were said to be

> the greatest curses of the metropolis. In them prostitution is carried on in a most unblushing manner under the thin cover of a legitimate business. They are in every instance conducted by the lowest order of women from whom all sense of decency, all traces of beauty, and all vestige of modesty has gone. In front of the dirty little shanties, a beggarly display of cigars and fruits is made while behind is a sitting room containing some gay furniture and a wheezy organ, or jingling piano is found, while several asthmetic [sic] painted females are prepared to sing or play cards. These places are hells, if there are any on earth.[14]

While "sewing girls" and "cigar stores" existed, brothels accounted for a major portion of the city's prostitutes. In an 1874 lecture about venereal disease, Dr. Stone, a local physician, estimated "that there were six regular houses in St. Paul with 36 inmates, and six irregular ones, such as cigar stores, with nine inmates who have rooms by themselves, and from 40 to 50 'kept women.'"[15] Three years later, there were eight brothels with fewer than fifty inmates, but reformers argued "there are in the city several hundreds of prostitutes, who are working an inexplicable evil."[16] This vague figure probably exaggerated the proportion of prostitutes outside the brothels. In 1883, Mayor Christopher O'Brien stated that the city had twelve regular brothels with sixty-four inmates, nine other houses with three to six inmates each, and "the usual number of the lower grades of disreputable women."[17]

Estimates of the numbers of prostitutes were subject to inaccuracies, especially regarding streetwalkers, who could not be counted accurately. However, St. Paul seems to have experienced a relatively steady demand for vice. Unlike new frontier communities, it was an established city without a severe shortage of women to inflate the demand for prostitution; in 1880, 49.5 percent of the population was female. The city's population increase following the Civil War was reflected in the accompanying rise in the number of brothels. Table 2.1 demonstrates that the ratio of brothels to city population remained relatively constant throughout this period. Police records show that five houses were in operation in 1886, seven in 1870, ten in 1874, and thirteen the following year, then dropping to ten in 1878 (in response to an antivice crusade), before reaching fourteen in 1880.[18]

St. Paul lacked a formally designated vice district, but most brothels were concentrated in two areas. Downtown, they clustered along and near four blocks of Fifth Street, running from Cedar to Sibley. The establishments "under the hill" were on or near Eagle Street, at the bottom of the bluffs, a few blocks southwest of downtown. Both

Table 2.1
Growth in City Population and Number of Brothels
in St. Paul, 1866–80

Year	No. of Brothels	Population	No. of People per Brothel
1866	5	12,886[a]	2,577
1870	7	20,030	2,861
1875	13	33,178	2,552
1880	14	41,473	2,962

Sources: Police records; federal censuses for 1870 and 1880; state censuses for 1865 and 1875.

[a]1865 population.

neighborhoods offered other forms of vice; in addition to brothels and "cigar stores," they contained notorious saloons, gambling "hells," and assignation houses (which rented rooms to couples). Public drunkenness and fights were commonplace. By 1882, the district "under the hill" was patrolled by both a regular patrolman and a special officer paid by the district's businesses. Not all brothels were in the vice districts; Mary E. Robinson's notorious house was located about two blocks north of the downtown area, and other houses were on the outskirts of the city.

Vice, then, had a modest place in St. Paul. The city lacked a large, nationally notorious vice district like those found in New York, New Orleans, and San Francisco, but prostitution was present. Local physicians spoke of the danger of venereal disease, local clergymen preached against tolerating sin, and residents of the city's respectable neighborhoods worried about the proximity of vice. In response, St. Paul's police had to use their limited resources to control prostitution. They solved this problem by using their arrest powers to establish a policy of regulation.

Regulation by Arrests

St. Paul began regulating vice in 1863. Prostitution was illegal under both Minnesota law and St. Paul's City Ordinance No. 10. These measures were apparently subject to irregular enforcement until 1863, when city officials devised a systematic method of applying the city ordinance. Under the new plan, the madams of St. Paul's brothels appeared before the police court once each month on charges of violating Ordinance No. 10 and paid a fine. This arrangement was public; officials repeatedly explained and defended the system in the newspapers during the years it was in operation. The plan was limited to the city's established brothels; madams operating "cigar stores" and independent prostitutes were not subject to regular arrests under the system. However, the police also enforced laws against streetwalking and arrested prostitutes for flagrant behavior in public places; independent prostitutes arrested on these charges faced relatively severe penalties, including jail sentences or being ordered to leave St. Paul. Thus, police supervised the established brothels through regular arrests of their madams while forcing prostitutes unaffiliated with the brothels to be discreet or risk harsh punishment.[19]

The mechanics of the regulatory system were simple. A woman who wanted to open a brothel visited the police chief and asked his permission, which was given if the "applicant was a proper person to inaugurate and carry on that business."[20] Inmates who joined houses also signed the "roll" at police headquarters. Each month, the madams appeared in the police court (later the municipal court). The courtroom procedures changed occasionally, but few months went by without the women appearing in court. During most months, each madam was fined either a fixed sum (e.g., $50) or a fixed sum plus an additional amount for each inmate (e.g., $25 plus $10 per inmate). Although the system did not require medical inspections, a woman presenting a note from a physician saying that she had been ill and unable to work during the past month was exempt from a fine. In some months, inmates were also ordered to appear in court, and the madams and inmates were fined individually, although the madam customarily paid her inmates' fines. During the madams' monthly appearances, everyone present observed the courtroom ritual: each madam came before the judge, heard the charge, and pled not guilty; the police chief was sworn in to testify to the disreputable character of the woman's house; and the judge gave a guilty verdict and levied a fine. City officials were careful to deny that the brothels were licensed; the law, they pointed out, prohibited vice. Nonetheless, the newspapers often referred to brothel "licenses," and none of the madams operating under this system ever received a jail sentence, although Ordinance No. 10 provided for fines up to $100 and jail terms of up to thirty days. St. Paul's police used these arrests to regulate, rather than prohibit, vice.[21]

This system of regulation through regular arrests was not exceptional. Like St. Paul, the Kansas cattle towns regulated vice through regular arrests during the 1870s and 1880s, as did Minneapolis, Toledo, and many other cities near the turn of the century. Three late-nineteenth-century surveys of police departments reveal the widespread use of policies for the regulation of vice rather than its eradication. Table 2.2 is adapted from the 1880 census. Each urban police department was asked to report the number of houses of prostitution in its city. In each geographic region, the modal response was to give a number, ranging from 1 to 517 (in Philadelphia). Outside of the northeastern states, less than 10 percent of the cities of over ten thousand population claimed to be free of brothels; roughly 75 percent acknowledged having at least one.[22] (St. Paul listed only

Table 2.2

**Police Departments' Responses to a Question about the Number
of Brothels in Their Cities, 1880 (cities over 10,000 population)**

Department's Response	Geographic Region			
	Northeast	North Central	South	West
"None"	31.4%	6.9%	3.2%	—
Gave Number	40.2%	72.4%	74.2%	80.0%
No Answer[a]	28.4%	20.7%	22.6%	20.0%
Total	100.0%	100.0%	100.0%	100.0%
N	102	58	31	10

Source: U.S. Census Office, Tenth Census, *Report on the Defective, Dependent, and Delinquent Classes* (Washington, D.C. 1888), table 136, pp. 566–70.

[a]Includes only those departments answering other questions; does not include 26 departments that did not respond to the survey.

seven brothels, although fourteen madams were regularly arrested during 1880.) While the numbers of brothels listed were probably inaccurate estimates, the police departments' willingness to report any brothels in their cities is evidence that they did not claim to have effective policies for prohibiting vice. In the comparable figures from the 1890 census, a similar pattern emerges, with roughly a third of the northeastern cities and over half of those in the rest of the country responding that they had at least one brothel. Again, the fact that police departments admitted to the presence of brothels in their cities suggests a degree of official toleration.[23]

Evidence from a third survey supports the conclusion that many cities regulated vice through arrests. For the 1893 edition of his *Police and Prison Cyclopedia,* George W. Hale wrote police chiefs asking, among other items, whether their cities "licensed" prostitutes. Most chiefs responded that they did not, but several added comments that revealed that they were defining licensing in the narrowest terms, and that their forces regulated vice in less formal ways:

There are ten recognized houses of prostitution in this city that may be called first-class of their kind; and there are quite a number of smaller houses about the city, confined principally to the colored persuasion, the character of which houses may be put down as doubtful. . . . There are no rules or regulations applying to houses of prostitution in this city, and they are not licensed. [Savannah]

When they get "foxy" we clean them out and allow a new crew to come in. [Appleton, Wisconsin]

I regulate them. So long as they are orderly they remain; if disorderly I raid their houses and drive them out of town. Knowing this, they do not give us much trouble. [Atlantic City]

Must not be on street after 9, enter saloons, ride carriage at night, flaunt avocation, no minors. [Memphis]

If they go where they are not wanted, or if persons are robbed in their houses, or if they make themselves too conspicuous, they are arrested and fined for being "keepers or inmates." [St. Louis]

Some departments noted that the women were arrested monthly, quarterly, or every four months. Unfortunately, by phrasing his question in terms of licensing, Hale only learned about other regulatory policies when a police chief saw fit to mention them. The chief of police in Lebanon, Pennsylvania, reported, "Do not know anything about houses of prostitution in this moral community"; about half the chiefs in northeastern cities and a quarter of those elsewhere said their cities had no brothels. Aside from these explicit denials, most chiefs simply reported that their cities did not license prostitutes—a response that clearly cannot be read as evidence of a policy aimed at prohibiting vice.[24] Without specifying the policies adopted by the majority of police forces, the three surveys suggest that St. Paul's informal policy of regulation, grounded in the police force's arrest powers, was not unusual. An examination of the workings of St. Paul's system of regulation reveals that such policies facilitated police efforts to maintain urban order.

Functions of Regulation

Newspaper stories about the madams' regular courtroom appearances sometimes included ironic comments about the city's financial interest in regulation: "Some of the recognized ladies of the city who keep houses for select gentlemen company in a very select manner, visited the City Hall yesterday. The haul of money was not large."[25] In fact, the system did generate a substantial proportion of the fines collected by St. Paul's lower court. In the year ending

March 31, 1870, offenses related to prostitution accounted for only 6 percent of the arrests made by the St. Paul police, while the $2,350 in fines for prostitution-related offenses comprised over 49 percent of the money collected by the police court. Similarly, in the year ending May 31, 1881, prostitution accounted for 7 percent of the city's arrests but over 42 percent of the municipal court's fines.[26] While these figures might seem to reveal a substantial financial interest in the regulatory system, the sums collected from madams comprised an insignificant portion of the city's total budget. For example, the $2,350 charged vice offenders in 1870 was equivalent to less than a sixth of the police department's annual payroll. In this context, St. Paul's economic interest in regulating prostitution seems modest. City officials, who openly defended regulation, never publicly based their defense on economic grounds.

Instead, officials argued that regulation made it easier for the police to keep order. Prostitution was associated with theft, violence, and other forms of disorder; trouble frequently occurred in brothels. The men and women who met in brothels may have felt that they were on a moral holiday, outside the law's supervision. Many of the men were visitors to St. Paul who knew a disorderly spree there probably would not affect their reputations in their home communities. Moreover, the sale of alcohol was a profitable sideline for madams, customers often made their visits to a brothel the last stop after an evening of drinking, and many brothel inmates drank heavily, so there was a good chance that several of the people in any given brothel would be under the influence of alcohol. In such circumstances, several forms of trouble could develop. If regulation could not prevent these problems, at least it could help the police with their efforts to bring the disorder under control.

Charges of theft were the aftermath of many nights in brothels. In some cases, prostitutes devised routines for robbing customers. Georgia Wright and her lover failed in one variation on the badger game. (In this racket, the lover, posing as an outraged husband, confronted the prostitute and her customer and tried to extort money from the victim.) Wright ran up a bill with a local merchant who appeared at her house to collect: "He had scarcely seated himself inside before a knock was heard at the door, and the virtuous housewife began to exhibit indications of fear. This surprised the gentleman, who wanted to know the cause of her alarm, and when he was informed that it was her husband who was knocking, he desired to know why in thunder it was that he did not open the door and come in."[27] Wright's intended victim complained to the police. In another instance, Henrietta Charles disrupted a badger game involving one of her inmates and the inmate's lover, interfering "simply on the ground that such practices would injure the reputation of her house."[28]

Badger games required some planning, but most thefts from customers probably developed spontaneously, when women saw the opportunity. Customers who complained to the police often were frustrated; madams and inmates usually denied that any theft had taken place, pointing out that the customer had been intoxicated and probably could not remember what had happened to his money. Customers who pursued their complaints and brought the women into court faced ridicule from the press: "William J. Connelly had commenced suit in the District Court against Miss Kate Hutton, for the purpose of recovering the sum of $285, which he claims this fair and beautiful lady got away from him sumhoweranuther."[29]

Not all thefts involved prostitutes stealing from customers. Sometimes the customer was the thief: "A man who is said to be a well-to-do merchant in Minneapolis came down from that city Saturday and stayed all night in the Bateson bagnio. Before retiring the girl took off her stocking, in which was $40 in money, and concealed it in the mattress. Surmising that it contained money the man got up early yesterday morning and securing it, decamped."[30] Customers also stole from each other; in one case, $500 was taken in this way.[31] Armed robbery was uncommon, but three men once entered Annie Oleson's brothel, intending to rob the establishment. Oleson and her inmates struggled with the robbers, the police were summoned, and the men fled.[32] Finally, thefts occurred among brothel residents; inmates occasionally charged their colleagues or madams with stealing. Since prostitutes often spent their earnings on jewelry, they were especially vulnerable to theft.[33]

Violence involving customers was common. Men occasionally stood outside a brothel, throwing stones at the building—particularly after a madam refused to admit them into her house.[34] There were several reports of madams suffering severe beatings from groups of men who entered the brothels.[35] The most celebrated incident involved Mary E. Robinson's charge that she was attacked and her brothel deliberately burned down by George Crummey. Arriving around midnight, Crummey and two friends demanded liquor and became abusive, with Crummey eventually beating Robinson; the

fire that destroyed her brothel began shortly thereafter. Disputes between inmates and customers also led to violence, including some
serious fights: "A man named Rose went into the house, and while
there began abusing a girl named Maud. She didn't like the abuse and
spoke spitefully to Rose. He continued his abuse, and several times
spat upon the girl. The latter left the room and went up stairs, where
she procured a small dagger and returned to the apartment below,
when Rose renewed the abuse, which caused Maud to whip out the
dagger and go for him. She slashed at him right and left, cutting him
six times in the right shoulder and once in the left wrist."[36]

Violence also marked internal relationships among brothel residents. Georgia Wright's willingness to fight earned her the nickname "Fighting Georgie." Inmates fought among themselves; other
incidents involved madams, pimps, and servants as combatants.
The press paid special attention to feuds between brothels, playfully
describing them in military language: "William C. Baker and wife,
alias Mollie McGuire, and Carrie McCarty, part of the garrison of
Fort Charles, were arraigned on charge of having tarred Fort Wright,
a rival establishment."[37] These interbrothel feuds reflected competition in the illicit marketplace; they sometimes began when a popular inmate moved from one brothel to another and the keeper of
the first house tried to get the inmate to return.

Brothel disorders were not limited to instances of theft and violence. Police were called in to deal with other problems involving
prostitutes. Fugitives sometimes hid in brothels after committing
serious crimes. (In some cases, the fugitive was a pimp who sought
refuge with his prostitute.) Police also entered brothels to investigate charges of white slavery, although these were relatively uncommon and only rarely substantiated, since most inmates joined
brothels voluntarily (see chapter 3). Finally, citizens demanded police action when brothels began operating in respectable neighborhoods. These complaints did not always involve a new brothel invading an established residential district. Several of St. Paul's
established brothels were built on the outskirts of the city, but, as
the city expanded, their locations became desirable property for
more respectable uses. In these cases, complainants sought to remove vice from its traditional location. Typically, these respectable
citizens were satisfied if the women agreed to move; the complainants wanted vice segregated, not eradicated.[38]

In short, there were many occasions when the police confronted disorder in the brothels, and St. Paul's policy of regulation helped them cope with these problems. The policy gave madams what was, in effect, a license to operate an illicit business. Retention of this license depended upon the madam's ability to minimize trouble and maintain order in her disorderly house. Brothels that became known as trouble spots were closed: "The chief of police yesterday closed up Kate Smith's house. . . . For some time this house has been the scene of violent and disgraceful disturbances, and some men who have been unwise enough to go there have been robbed of considerable sums of money."[39] Even madams of well-established houses could be forced out of business; Kate Hutton had managed her brothel for fourteen years when the mayor ordered it closed in 1880 on the grounds that she was drinking heavily and no longer keeping order in the house.[40] A single serious offense also could lead to a house being closed; when police learned that Carrie Moore had tried to first trick and then force two young girls to join her house, the brothel was ordered closed.[41] Even "cigar stores," which were not regulated through monthly arrests, were shut down when they became too disorderly. Short of closing a brothel, police could single out troublesome prostitutes and order them to leave St. Paul. Maud Murdock, the prostitute who attacked an abusive customer with a dagger, became involved in a series of disorderly incidents and was finally ordered out of town by the chief of police.[42]

Similarly, while the police ordinarily did not try to reform prostitutes, they cooperated with parents trying to rescue their daughters from brothels:

> To all the entreaties of her mother to abandon her present mode of life she replied with scorn and contempt, and utterly refused to go with her. The chief then told her that if this was her determination she would have to leave town on the next train for she should not under any circumstances stay in any house of ill-fame in St. Paul. This was a determination of the matter that she had not looked for and brought the young lady to her senses. Finally, after many tears and much weeping she consented to go with her mother, and the two left the chief's office together, the chief having reiterated to her that she would not be allowed to remain in this city if she endeavored to remain in any of the houses spoken of.[43]

While the police could coerce a madam's cooperation by threatening to close her house, they also could help protect her from some of the dangers inherent in her business. When two would-be customers forced their way into Annie Oleson's brothel, she "at once sent word to the police headquarters and an officer was dispatched to the scene."[44] Three weeks earlier, Oleson had called for the police during the attempted robbery of her house. Their quasi-legitimate status under regulation may have made madams more willing to summon the police when disorders broke out, as a means of minimizing trouble. Madams and prostitutes felt free to bring formal charges against customers (and one another) for assault, theft, passing counterfeit money, and so forth. Madams usually cooperated with police who entered their houses to stop fights, investigate complaints, or search for fugitives. By cooperating, madams could gain the authorities' good will at little or no cost to themselves; in some cases, they clearly benefited from police intervention that restored order in their brothels.[45]

Madams also benefited from regulation in less direct ways. In addition to offering them police protection from predatory customers and colleagues, the city's policy offered a promise of long-term stability. Some St. Paul brothels operated at the same address for over ten years with minimal interference. Madams cemented their working relationships with the authorities in various ways. The newspapers hinted that brothel customers included prominent businessmen as well as state and local officials—men who could use their influence to protect the brothels. Occasionally, these men were said to supply the money to pay a madam's fine. The motive behind such support might have been gratitude or, as the press sometimes speculated, fear of blackmail. Madams also befriended the police, who were invited to open-house parties at Christmastime or on the occasion of a new brothel's opening. One brief newspaper item hinted that the police could exploit the opportunities open to them: "It is reported that there are a good many applicants for the position of special policeman to watch the houses of ill-fame. They all calculate on dead-head passes and blackmailing."[46] These ties with officials, coupled with the brothels' quasi legitimacy under the regulatory system, made the madams' operations relatively secure and safe.

St. Paul's system of regulation functioned to minimize disorder. It helped the police control the problems associated with prostitution and gave madams reason to cooperate with police efforts. If the authorities assumed that prostitution was inevitable, they did not believe that it had to be troublesome. The system of regulation was judged by whether the brothels were orderly; the newspapers made it clear that order was the objective: "The police are going to keep a more strict eye upon the improper houses in St. Paul. Any irregularities of conduct that are seen will cause them to be closed up."[47] Again, after one madam sued another over a rent payment, the *Pioneer Press* ignored the fact that brothels were illegal when declaring: "At the best, these courtesans and their habituations are nuisances, and the women become doubly such when they force their unseemly personal squabbles upon the courts for adjudication. If these 'mesdames' cannot keep themselves as much as possible from the public gaze, the mayor will be perfectly justified in closing up the establishments of those who compel public recognition of them."[48]

Summary

As "*the* social evil," prostitution loomed larger in the nation's consciousness during the late nineteenth century than in any other period. Prostitution became the focus of many nineteenth-century debates about urban policy. Experts agreed that vice was a major problem, but they disagreed about the problem's nature. Physicians emphasized the threat to public health and clergymen objected to immorality, although ordinary citizens rarely became vocal unless vice infringed on their lives and homes. The debate's participants also disagreed over the philosophical basis for social control policy. For some—particularly physicians and city officials—a policy had to be practical; if vice could not be prohibited, it should be regulated. Following Sanger's lead, regulation's advocates pointed to prostitution's long history; since antiquity, vice had continued to exist, in spite of all efforts to prohibit it. In contrast, clergymen and other reformers argued for principled policies; a determined effort to prohibit vice might succeed, and even if it did not, by making such an effort a community adopted the morally correct posture. Regulation's fundamental flaw was that it compromised with evil. This conflict between advocates of practical compromise and defenders of moral principle continued throughout the late nineteenth and early twentieth centuries. The debate ranged far beyond St. Paul; it was nationwide, although the policies adopted varied from city to city.

In many cities, the police resolved the debate by establishing de facto policies of regulation. However, regulation must have worked best in cities of modest size, such as St. Paul, where the number of brothels was relatively small and streetwalking could be kept to a minimum. Authorities in larger cities probably could not keep track of the bigger populations of prostitutes well enough to manage the bookkeeping that regulation through arrests required.

Experts on each side of this debate assumed that the police were the appropriate agents for controlling vice. Yet police could not simply follow the policymakers' orders; they had their own concerns. Both the threat of disease and the issue of morality paled before the police force's need to maintain order. In particular, the police knew they had limited control over the illicit marketplace for vice: they had no way of ending the demand for sexual services or halting the supply of young women seeking the independence and income that prostitution promised. Prohibition was beyond their power, but they could regulate vice and, in doing so, keep the illicit marketplace relatively orderly. For the police, the question was not whether St. Paul would have prostitution, but what form it would take. Could it be restricted to certain areas within the city? Could the women operate as streetwalkers or out of brothels, "cigar stores," or private rooms? Could young women be protected from being forced or tricked into entering prostitution? Could customers and prostitutes be protected from theft and violence? Could respectable citizens be protected from the offending sights and sounds of vice? Could innocent third parties be protected from venereal disease? St. Paul's system for regulation was designed to address some of these questions. It located prostitution as a quasi-legitimate industry within the city. As a practical matter, regulation served to segregate vice and give the police access to the brothels, thereby minimizing disorder and maximizing police control over the illicit marketplace. Under the system, madams paid regular fines; while this increased the city's income, it was not the policy's major function.[49] Rather, regulation maintained a stable marketplace for vice, and that stability was in the best interests of the police, many respectable citizens, and the women who passed through St. Paul's brothels.

3

CAREERS IN
BROTHEL PROSTITUTION

In his 1871 discourse on "the social problem," Reverend A. A. E. Taylor described the fate of a typical prostitute:

> "Seest thou this woman?" To-day, painted and bedecked with finery, bold and brazen, gay and gaudy, she sails by your doors, recklessly flaunting the flag of Satan in your very faces; next year, hiding away, dispirited, soured, clinging to the faded tatters of her former pride, venturing out in the night-time, her mouth full of cursing and bitterness, her heart a canker, her retreat a cellar or a loft; the third year you shall find her in the lowest dens of degradation, a drunkard, wretched, despairing, among sailors and the worst criminal classes, none so low as to do her reverence, abused and abandoned of God and man; the next year you shall find an unsodded grave, with no headstone, no epitaph—one small mound in a row, where, in the Potter's field, side by side, out of sight, they lay the Magdalenes.[1]

Taylor was not alone in believing that prostitutes moved through a series of increasingly shabby circumstances, dying within a few years. In 1858, Dr. William Sanger surveyed two thousand New York prostitutes; the vast majority reported they had been in prostitution for less than five years. This finding, coupled with his assumption that respectable society would never readmit a fallen woman, led to Sanger's ingenuous conclusion that most prostitutes died within four years. Like Taylor, he argued that the women were downwardly mobile; although they might start in elite brothels, they inevitably descended to disease, drunkenness, and death.[2]

These descriptions might have amused Mary E. Robinson. In 1874, she responded to one of St. Paul's reformers' crusades against vice by informing the press she was retiring. After auctioning her brothel's contents, she remained in the city, supervising her substantial real estate holdings. Apparently, she continued to do well. When she died at the age of eighty-two, she was buried under a massive stone, on a prime lot in a local cemetery.[3] Robinson appears to fit one of the stock roles in the myth of Victorian prostitution: the shrewd madam who saved her earnings, invested wisely, and retired to a life of comfort. Few life stories stand in clearer contradiction to the picture drawn by Taylor and Sanger.

Obviously, Robinson was exceptional, but authorities disagree over whether the typical nineteenth-century prostitute died in misery or returned to respectability. Unlike Sanger, Dr. William Acton, Victorian England's leading medical expert on vice, believed that most prostitutes "return sooner or later to a more or less regular course of life." This debate continues among modern historians. Frances Finnegan's study of York streetwalkers concludes that women entered prostitution because they were poor and that they found drink, disease, and destitution rather than opportunities for improvement. In contrast, Judith and Daniel Walkowitz argue, "even for the most notorious prostitutes . . . streetwalking was a transitional stage that they would pass through."[4] In this view, women drifted in and out of prostitution according to their circumstances; many eventually left vice for respectable employment or marriage. While the majority of prostitutes remained poor, they were not doomed to special misery, and a few were upwardly mobile.

The sociological concept of the deviant career can clarify the issues in this debate. In an influential essay, Howard S. Becker defined career as "the sequence of movements from one position to another in an occupational system made by any individual who works in that system."[5] Adapting the concept to the study of deviance, Becker outlined four stages in the deviant career: committing a deviant act; acquiring a deviant perspective; being caught and labeled; and joining a deviant group. Becker's essay became the standard statement of the interactionist or labeling theory of deviance, but other sociologists have criticized his description of the deviant career for being overly rigid. Edward Sagarin asks: "Is the career the same for all [deviant] groups, or do they have in common only the fact of career? Within each group, can common threads of development be found, which many or most individuals will follow? Or, on the other hand, are there many pathways once one has taken the first step, and in fact are there many different first steps? And do some of these paths lead 'backward,' away from the ultimate identity with the deviant way?"[6]

Similarly, Edwin M. Lemert notes that, while respectable bureaucracies tightly structure the careers of their employees, deviants have more options: "The flux and pluralism of modern society make concepts of drift, contingency, and risk far more meaningful in deviance than inevitability or linear progress. A more defensible conception of deviant career is that of recurrent or typical contingencies and problems awaiting someone who continues in a course of action, with the added notion that there may be theoretically 'best' choices set into a situation by prevailing technology and social structure."[7] In short, career patterns can vary within a deviant group; while some individuals take common pathways into, through, and out of deviance, others may blaze new trails. The single-minded models that describe prostitutes' careers in terms of either downward mobility or reentry into respectability ignore the various options open to the women.

In nineteenth-century St. Paul, the deviant careers of women engaged in brothel prostitution followed various routes. In this respect, St. Paul was typical of many other cities. Its prostitutes made career choices—to enter or leave vice, to move from brothel to brothel or city to city, and between the statuses of madam and prostitute—that were available to prostitutes elsewhere. The picture that emerges is one of women in motion, choosing among the available career paths, within the confines posed by the respectable community's economy and morality and the underworld's structure.

Madams, Brothels, and Inmates

St. Paul's system of regulation distinguished between madams and the inmates who worked in their brothels. After 1867, madams brought before the police court (later the municipal court) were charged with keeping a house of ill fame, while inmates ordinarily faced charges of visiting a house of ill fame. The same charge, violating Ordinance No. 10, was made against both categories of women before 1868, but the fines were different; madams paid from $15 to over $100, prostitutes only $10.[8] Madams also were distinguished by their regular monthly appearances in the city's courtroom where they were charged and fined. During some months, inmates were required to appear in court with the madams, sometimes being charged separately, but often as part of a brothel's "family." On such occasions, madams paid a fixed fine plus an additional fee for each inmate; typically, a madam paid $25 plus $10 per prostitute. In other months, the madams appeared in court unaccompanied, each paying a single, larger sum, that sometimes took into account the number of prostitutes in her house. Regardless of the system of fines adopted by the court in a given month, the madam apparently paid all of the fines for her brothel.[9]

As a consequence of this policy, madams can be identified by their regular appearances in the court records. If a madam is defined as a person who was either charged with keeping a house of ill fame or charged with violating Ordinance No. 10 and fined more than $10, on at least three occasions during one calendar year, then forty madams can be identified between November 1865 and May 1883 (see appendix). Demographic information is available for nineteen of these women. Thirteen reported being born in the United States; one each was born in England, Scotland, Ireland, Germany, and Sweden, and one madam's nativity was not given. Nine reported being single, while seven said they were married, and there was no information regarding three. Of the married women, at least two lived with their husbands in their brothels; one of these men, Sarah Kimball's husband, George, sometimes faced charges of keeping a house of ill fame. Unlike the stereotypical middle-aged madam, the women were young; age at first known arrest as a madam ranged from twenty to forty, with a median of only twenty-six. Similarly, the age at the last known arrest as a madam ranged from twenty-two to forty-eight, with a median age of twenty-eight.[10]

The forty madams accumulated 1,029 known arrests for prostitution, including arrests as madams, brothel inmates, and independent prostitutes.[11] The number of arrests per woman ranged from

3 to 109, with a median of 15.5 (and a mean of 25.7). Sarah Kimball and her husband George had only 17 arrests, but they spanned a sixteen-year period, 1866-81. This spotty record may reflect their location at Oneida and James Streets during most of the period—well away from downtown and the police. Then, too, the Kimballs may have drifted in and out of brothel keeping; in various city directories, George was listed as a painter, glass stainer, and laborer, while Sarah was once recorded as doing washing and ironing. Kate Hutton's career was nearly as long (1867-81) and more consistent, with 109 arrests over almost fifteen years. Annie Oleson had the most consecutive arrests; she was charged in 62 of the 63 months from May 1875 to July 1880. While her string of routine arrests was exceptional, twenty-one madams had at least 10 arrests in one twelve-month period. The city's records, although incomplete, reveal considerable stability in the madams' careers.

Brothel locations displayed even greater stability. Addresses are known for thirty-two of the madams.[12] Often, one madam succeeded another in managing the same brothel; altogether, the thirty-two women operated twenty firms. (See appendix.) Thirteen firms had only one known madam; Robinson, who ran her brothel for over eight years, had the longest tenure. At the other extreme, the "Lookout," at 1 Jackson Street, operated for ten years under eight different madams. One firm was especially stable; a brothel operated at 94 Washington Street from 1865 to 1883, under the management of four madams; when the original house burned down in 1876, another was built on the lot within a year.

Firms displayed different patterns of operation. Several moved from one building to another. When Lou Adams registered with the police in September 1873, she gave her address as 14 Washington Street, "under the hill" near several other brothels. Six months later, she had moved to 11 Nash Street—located in a respectable neighborhood—but neighbors' complaints drove her out. By the end of 1874, her brothel was located downtown, near Cedar and Third Streets—her third address in sixteen months. Some madams bought their buildings and rented them to their successors. Kate Hutton bought the house at 7 Hill Street in 1869 and ran the establishment until 1875. She left to live with her lover, and Maggie Morse took over for a year, presumably paying Hutton rent. When Hutton returned, Morse moved into the rebuilt house at 94 Washington

Street, establishing one of the finest brothels in the city. By 1879, she was in turn renting her building to Jennie Bateson. In two cases, firms merged. Thus, Florence Campbell ran the brothel at 93 Eagle Street from 1870 until she became ill in 1877. Then Hattie McBride, who operated a "cigar store" at 71 Robert Street, took over the Eagle Street house.[13]

Although St. Paul's madams and their brothels remain visible in historical records, less can be determined about the brothels' inmates. Besides the established madams, several hundred other people were arrested on prostitution charges between 1865 and 1883, including madams of minor, short-lived establishments, brothel inmates, independent prostitutes, pimps, servants, and customers. Unfortunately, it is frequently impossible to determine the category to which an individual belonged. In particular, because visiting a house of ill fame was an all-purpose prostitution charge, brothel inmates cannot be distinguished from independent prostitutes or inmates of "cigar stores." Positive identification of brothel inmates is only possible in two sources: structured arrest records that list inmates beneath their respective madams, and manuscript census schedules. The most detailed set of structured arrest records appeared in the arrest ledger between April and October 1873; sixty-one prostitutes were listed as brothel inmates during those months. Inmates from six brothels appeared in census schedules; three brothels in 1870, two in 1880, and one in the state census of 1875 listed a total of thirty inmates. Two women appeared in both the structured records and a census schedule, so a total of eighty-nine inmates can be identified from both sources.[14]

Demographically, the inmates resembled the madams. Their ages ranged from sixteen to thirty, with a median of twenty-two; twenty-three were under twenty-one, fifty-one were between twenty-one and twenty-five, and ten were over twenty-five (ages were unrecorded for five women). Of the fifty-six for whom marital status is known, fifty-five were single. Over three-quarters were native-born: sixty-seven from the United States; three each from Canada, Ireland, and Sweden; two from Germany; one each from England, France, and Italy; with eight unknown. Census schedules gave the state of birth for twenty-four native-born women; eighteen (75 percent) came from only five states—Minnesota, New York, Wisconsin, Illinois, and Pennsylvania. (The same states accounted for 79 percent of the native-born residents in the 1880 federal census of St. Paul.) Compared to their madams, brothel inmates were slightly younger, somewhat less likely to be married, but about equally likely to have been born in the United States.[15] If geographic and cultural differences are taken into account, this pattern resembles those found in other studies of nineteenth-century prostitutes.[16]

Brothels tended to fluctuate in size from month to month, but a typical establishment had four to six inmates in residence plus the madam. Sometimes brothels were quite small; the Kimballs had only two "dressmakers" living with them in 1880, and Cora Webber had only one prostitute (as well as a handful of other men and women) in her house in 1870. At the other extreme, Mary E. Robinson had ten inmates with her in 1870, and Hattie McBride had nine in 1880.[17]

The structural context for brothel prostitution in St. Paul between 1865 and 1883 is relatively clear. The police supervised the brothels but let them operate openly. Most firms were located in well-established vice districts, where brothels could attract customers with minimal interference, sometimes operating from the same building for several years. The brothels were small, managed by women who often had stable careers as madams. The women involved in brothel prostitution, both as madams and inmates, were typically in their twenties, single, and native-born. Within this structure, however, these women experienced fluid careers, finding their way into the world of vice, changing locations and sometimes statuses, and ultimately leaving prostitution.

Entering Prostitution

Most sociologists studying deviant careers focus on the initial step—becoming deviant. For theoretical and practical reasons, it is important to ask why some people turn to prostitution or other forms of deviance. Interactionist studies of deviant careers argue that, in addition to committing their first deviant acts, individuals entering deviance must modify their definition of self, redefining deviance as an appropriate activity and justifying their involvement in it. For some, deviance may be a defense against a threat, while others may seek adventure through deviance; in any case, entry into deviance involves assessing options and, ultimately, choosing deviance.[18]

Other explanations assign the individual a less active role in the process of becoming deviant; in these models, the person becomes a pawn of outside forces. Prostitutes fascinated the Victorians, who wanted to understand why women entered vice. Nineteenth-century sexual ideology favored explanations that denied that prostitution was a calculated choice. Medical and scientific literature, as well as popular writings, minimized female sexuality and emphasized women's innocence and purity. Since purity was woman's essence, prostitution represented a fundamental contradiction—purity depraved. This contradiction accounts for the explanations for prostitution favored by nineteenth-century moralists. Reformers pointed to the white-slave trade's role in ruining young girls; innocents were said to be abducted and forced to enter brothels or they were tricked into beginning a "life of shame."[19]

These accounts protected the myth of female purity by blaming evil procurers, rather than the prostitute, for the woman's fall into vice, thereby casting the woman entering prostitution in the role of victim. However, once a woman became committed to vice, moralists redefined her as no longer innocent, instead viewing her as depraved, a "sinister polluter" who preyed on young men. Other contemporary explanations suggest that women entered vice because of a weakness in their character: loving "not wisely but too well," they were seduced; permitted to read novels, they became corrupted by false, romantic ideas; or, proud and greedy, they longed to wear fine clothes. Explanations of this sort let moralists acknowledge the existence of prostitution without denying the essential innocence and purity of women. Yet newspaper stories of the period revealed the inadequacy of these explanations and the ideology that lay behind them.

St. Paul's newspapers shared the Victorian fascination with women's descent into vice, but they offered little support for claims that abduction or trickery led women into prostitution. To be sure, prostitutes occasionally accounted for their "fall" in this fashion, and their stories sometimes were believed. The president of St. Paul's Magdalen Home repeated one resident's sad tale: out of work and unable to find a job, she met a stranger who offered her food and lodging. She followed the woman to her home, but when she discovered the house was a brothel, "she was told it was no use now, for since she had slept under that roof, she was doomed—that no one would now believe but that she was a fallen woman."[20] The newspapers were alert for such stories of abducted or tricked women. When one young woman arrived in the city and told an elaborate story about being lured from her St. Louis home to a St. Paul brothel, reformers eagerly intervened. Although she proved surprisingly ignorant about St. Louis—unable even to describe the location of her home in relation to the river—she was given a ticket back.[21] In another case, an inmate, arrested in a drunken brothel disorder, created a stir by announcing that she was being held against her will. The authorities investigated but found her claim false.[22]

In fact, only three of the forty established madams were accused in the newspapers of acquiring new inmates by devious means, and only one of these claims was substantiated. Carrie Moore opened her brothel in August 1880 and was fined in three consecutive months. Near the end of October, she was charged with inveigling two young girls into her house and trying to force one to stay. The police promptly closed the house for good.[23] In an unsubstantiated case, a brothel inmate claimed to have been tricked into entering prostitution, while a newspaper charged that Kate Hutton was "in the habit of enticing innocent young girls to her den of infamy and treating them with ice cream and liquor and thereby winning their confidence, and seducing them from their parents, with the aim of educating them into her own vicious practices."[24] However, the inmate's story was debunked and the charges against Hutton forgotten. Similarly, rumors that Annie Oleson tricked a young girl into joining her brothel also were dispelled; the madam actually tried to discourage the girl, who wanted to enter the house, and convinced her to seek the protection of a priest.[25] Aside from the Moore case, the newspapers reported only four instances where evidence showed that young girls had been forced or tricked into prostitution; none of the four involved an established brothel, and in each case the authorities reacted by sentencing the procurers to jail.[26]

Madams looking for inmates did not need to resort to force or trickery. The madam of a "gunboat"—a floating brothel located downriver at Red Wing—came to St. Paul to recruit inmates. She began at the established brothels but could not interest any of their inmates in coming with her, so she recruited three adolescent girls. The officials stepped in before the four left town; brought before the police court, two girls repented and were sent home, while the third, still eager to go, was placed in a Chicago Magdalen asylum.[27] These stories sum up the limited evidence that a white-slave trade supplied inmates for St. Paul's brothels.

Other women entered prostitution after being seduced and abandoned by their lovers. As a pregnant, abandoned adolescent, Kate Hutton turned to prostitution.[28] The investigation of a brothel inmate's death following an abortion revealed a similar story.[29] In her 1878 report, the president of the Magdalen Home argued that "the girls who supply all the brothels are, in ninety-nine cases out of every hundred, those who have first been seduced."[30] Her predecessor explained the process: "Father or mother or both dying early, and left without a mother's love and care, becoming an easy prey to apparent love and sympathy. I think seven-tenths are of this class."[31] These estimates were probably high, affected by the Home's responsibility for all fallen women, especially unwed mothers. During the late nineteenth century, the term "prostitution" encompassed all illicit sexual liaisons, not merely those involving payment. Former brothel inmates did come to the Magdalen Home, but they formed only part of the clientele—not even all of those labeled prostitutes.

While there was limited support for romantic explanations for women's entry into prostitution via abduction, trickery, or seduction, these incidents lay outside the general pattern. According to newspaper accounts, the most common pathway into vice involved a calculated decision, reflecting the available opportunities for women in the city. Some young women, dominated by their parents, saw prostitution as a means of escaping unhappy family lives. Others, probably the majority, entered prostitution because it was one of the few ways a poor woman could earn a comfortable living. Working-class women were largely restricted to employment in the needle trades or domestic service, careers that offered few prospects and paid notoriously little. The 1880 census listed 3,081 St. Paul women in selected occupations; two categories—tailors, dressmakers, and milliners, and domestic servants—accounted for 77 percent of their jobs. Although there were reports of prostitutes whose parents were "very respectable" or even "wealthy," most women chose prostitution because it offered one of the few chances for a more comfortable life.[32]

One story, well designed to shock the Victorian reader with its theme of vice as a calculated choice, appeared repeatedly in the newspapers. In its simplest version, a young woman, usually fifteen to eighteen, leaves home and eventually enters a brothel. Sometimes the newspaper gave bits of her history: upon her father's death, her mother had to go to work, placing the children in other homes; or the young woman followed her sister into prostitution; or she was a frequent reader of "yellow covered novels, whose gross and prurient teachings have had their poisonous effect on her mind";[33] or, most commonly, she left her position as a domestic servant. One of her parents, another relative, or occasionally a city official or well-meaning citizen searches for her, finds her, and tries to convince her to give up her "life of shame." In virtually every case, the young woman resists. She gives various reasons: "She said she would never feel comfortable [living with a respectable family] and could never earn enough at her trade to dress as she desired to dress. . . . She had counted the costs, and was determined to remain and lead, if must be, a short but merry life of pleasure";[34] "she was treated so badly at home that she could not live there, and resorted to this disgraceful life as her only means of getting a living";[35] or "the daughter was hard, knowing, and obdurate, and evidently not at all disposed to abandon her life of excitement and gaiety, for the disheartening one of daily labor and a slavish life subject to the tyrannical orders of unfeeling mistresses."[36] Threatened with incarceration if she does not return to respectability, she sometimes complies, sometimes remains defiant: "She declared that it made no difference how long they sentenced her, when she got out she would go back to Eighth street again."[37] This story, which appeared in seventeen different versions, caused reporters considerable discomfort. Faced with a woman's clear, calculated choice of prostitution, the myth of female innocence could not be maintained. Instead, the young women were characterized in harsh terms: "The girl's action is explicable only on the ground of precocious perversity."[38]

Not every adolescent girl who tried to enter a brothel was admitted; madams discouraged or turned away some young applicants. Moreover, there were other routes into prostitution. Some women were born to the scarlet. Mary J. France, madam of one of St. Paul's finest brothels, had "associated with her in the nefarious business two daughters, both of whom have grown up in St. Paul, and the younger, who can scarcely be eighteen years of age, is known to be gradually but surely fading away to a consumptive's grave."[39] Others may have started out as servants in the brothels; the *Pioneer* discovered a fifteen-year old girl, whose mother received relief, working at Mary E. Robinson's house and wearing the madam's old clothing.[40] On other occasions, older women, already married, entered brothels. One woman left her husband of eleven years, a Minneapolis policeman, to enter Sarah Mason's house.[41] Another, married for three months, discovered that her husband expected her to support him and walked out, joining Nellie Otis's brothel.[42] Sometimes the husband played a more direct role; one young woman fled Minneapolis, joining her sister in a St. Paul brothel, after her husband tried to force her to prostitute herself.[43] Other reports mentioned women who were married to their pimps but did not say whether they entered prostitution under their husbands' direction.

Mobility in Prostitution

Once an individual embarks on a deviant career, new options become apparent. Over time, the individual may learn new skills, develop contacts with other deviants, or become aware of additional opportunities within deviance. Deviants may get several chances to alter the course of their careers.[44] Different career pathways were open to St. Paul's prostitutes. For economic as well as personal reasons, most prostitutes kept moving. Geographic mobility, from one city to another or between brothels in the same city, was very common. In addition, some women were upwardly mobile within the world of vice, changing status from brothel inmate to madam. Overall, the population of prostitutes was constantly shifting.

Movement to and from St. Paul was commonplace. For some women, moving to the city was part of the process of becoming a prostitute; a typical pattern had a young woman leave her hometown, travel to St. Paul and take a low-paying but respectable job as a waitress or domestic, and then enter a brothel after a few months. The news stories about parents hunting for their daughters spoke of young women from Faribault, Mankato, Shakopee, and other towns in Minnesota and Wisconsin. Others moved to St. Paul after becoming prostitutes. The register of prostitutes kept by the police was unsystematic, but it occasionally listed the place of origin or, less often, the destination of women leaving St. Paul. While some of those listed may have been newcomers to vice, many probably came from brothels elsewhere. As might be expected, many entries named towns in Minnesota or the surrounding region, including Minneapolis, Anoka, Duluth, Winona, and Brainerd. Other women were on the move to or from major cities in the eastern half of the country, including New York, Brooklyn, Buffalo, Detroit, Chicago, Milwaukee, Memphis, St. Louis, St. Joseph, Kansas City, and Omaha. Only one woman's origin was listed as outside the country—Norway. Sometimes madams deliberately imported inmates; in 1867, Mary E. Robinson brought four prostitutes from Chicago, although they left St. Paul after a couple of weeks, complaining that the customers were not as wealthy as those in Chicago.[45]

Most women probably had their own reasons for moving. The authorities ordered some prostitutes to leave the city. In 1878, Maud Murdock, a brothel inmate, knifed a customer. A few months later, after promising to reform, she appeared in the post office, trying to attract customers by wearing school girls' clothing. The chief of police ordered her out of town. The following spring, the newspapers reported that she had been seen, still in a girl's costume, first in Chicago and later in New York.[46] Similarly, Nellie Otis closed her St. Paul brothel and moved to Fargo because she was threatened with a prison sentence.[47] Just as St. Paul's authorities drove some women away, others came to the city fleeing officials elsewhere: "[one was] . . . kicked out of all the houses in St. Louis, where she has been for years, as a worn out piece of furniture, and totally unfit for that city, where houses of evil repute are under surveillance."[48] Not all pressure to move came from officials. When fire struck Chicago's vice district, five hundred prostitutes reportedly fled, some to St. Paul.[49]

While newspapers were more likely to cover these dramatic stories, most women probably moved simply because the opportunities seemed better elsewhere. The proximity of Minneapolis made it especially easy to shift cities; police raids or rumors of a crackdown occasionally led women to move across the Mississippi River into the other jurisdiction. Or a woman having bad luck in one city might decide to make the short move in order to improve her prospects. Even madams switched locations; Emma Dibble, who ran a brothel in St. Paul in 1865, moved her establishment to Minneapolis, then returned to St. Paul briefly in 1870.[50]

Once in St. Paul, brothel inmates often moved from one establishment to another. Reasons for changing houses varied; at least one prostitute alternated between Henrietta Charles's brothel and the "Cave House" on the outskirts of town.[51] Jennie Bork also moved to the Charles brothel after Mary E. Robinson's house burned down in 1869 but returned to her former firm when it reopened. Sometimes inmates left at the madam's orders; Bork testified at the Robinson arson trial that she heard someone going up to the attic (where the inmates stored their luggage) in the middle of the night, but "I supposed one of the girls had had a fuss and had got to go."[52] On other occasions, madams were angry when inmates left, particularly if the prostitute attracted customers. Minnie Gay left Henrietta Charles's house "very much to the disgust of the latter lady, who then became the looser [sic] of large numbers of greenbacks." Charles found Gay in the Cave House and assaulted her.[53] Similarly, Jennie Bateson and Clara Morton feuded over who should house a popular inmate.[54]

Mobility between cities and within St. Paul gave brothels shifting populations. Madams might remain at one address for years, but inmates rarely did. Jennie Bork, twenty-two years old, testified that she had been "living with Mrs. Robinson altogether for six years, though I have been away some of the time," and Kate Bailey lived in the Robinson brothel periodically from 1868 to 1872.[55] They were exceptions; most inmates moved on after a few months, particularly if the brothel they occupied was not under stable management.

Tables 3.1 and 3.2, drawn from the structured records in the arrest ledger for April to October 1873, illustrate the high rate of turnover. Kate Hutton's brothel, shown in table 3.1, had the same madam for several years. During those seven months in 1873, thirteen prostitutes were arrested as inmates of the house, with between one and seven arrests apiece. In addition, two of these women were arrested as inmates of other brothels during this period. A third prostitute had an arrest as an independent, that is, she did not appear in court on the same day as the brothel inmates and was presumably working on her own. These arrest records should have been relatively complete; each woman paid a fine, giving the authorities an interest in arresting every inmate. The brothel fluctuated in size from four to seven inmates; counting Hutton, between four and six of the women arrested each month had been

Table 3.1
Arrests in Kate Hutton's Brothel, April–October 1873

	Date of Arrest							
Woman	Apr. 10	May 13	June 12	July 11	Aug. 13	Sept. 10	Oct. 4	Arrests per person
Kate Hutton	K	K	K	K	K	K	K	7
Carrie McCarthy	V	V	V	V	V	V	D	7
Annie Oleson	V	D		D	D	D	D	6
Mollie Whitney	V	V	V			O_1	O_1	3
Lizzie Snowhill	V	V	V					3
Josephine Marshall	V	V		V				3
Eve Steward		V	V	V	V	V		5
Blanche Fuller	I	V	V			V	V	4
Grace Clark			V	V				2
Tina Clark				V				1
Hattie Roberts				V				1
Julie Westlake					V	V		2
Nelly Cook			O_2	O_2	O_2	V		1
Ella Brown						V	D	2
Total	6	8	7	8	5	8	5	47

Notes: Totals include only arrests within this brothel. K = arrest for "Keeping a House of Ill Fame," $20 fine; V = arrest under Hutton for "Visiting a House of Ill Fame," $10 fine; D = arrest under Hutton for "Visiting a House of Ill Fame," dismissed; O = arrest under another madam for "Visiting a House of Ill Fame" (subscripts denote different brothels); I = (independent) arrest for "Visiting a House of Ill Fame" but not listed under a madam (on an odd day of the same month).

there the previous month. This reflects a reasonably stable population within the establishment; occupants tended to remain from one month to the next.

In contrast, table 3.2 shows the arrest pattern in a second, less stable house. This brothel, the "Lookout," located at 1 Jackson, had four madams during the seven-month period; control passed from Lizzie Warren, who had run the house for six months, temporarily into the hands of Minnie Brown and Stella Austin, before Kate Bailey took over for about a year. Six other women were arrested as inmates of this brothel; none had more than five arrests in the seven months. This establishment had considerable turnover; the number of occupants who remained in the brothel from one month to the next ranged from only one to three. While Hutton's brothel was a relatively large, relatively stable establishment, the house at 1 Jackson was smaller and considerably less stable.

Table 3.2
Arrests in Brothel at 1 Jackson, April–October 1873

	Date of Arrest							Arrests per person
Woman	Apr. 9	May 13	June 12	July 10	Aug. 13	Sept. 10	Oct. 4	
Lizzie Warren	K							1
Minnie Brown		K	V					2
Stella Austin	V	V	K	K				4
Kate Bailey	V	V			K	K	K	5
Mollie Slantry	V							1
Louisa Johnson		V	V	V	V		V	5
Georgia Austin		V	V	V	V	V		5
Lillie Thompson	O_1	O_1		V	I	O_2	O_2	1
Mary Hudson					V	V		2
Jo Johnson						V		1
Total	4	4	4	4	4	4	2	26

Notes: Totals include only arrests within this brothel. See table 3.1 for key.

The cumulative impact of these shifting populations, even in the relatively stable houses, was to repopulate the city's brothels every few months. Although the data are limited because brothel inmates were not arrested systematically during most months, comparisons can be drawn between the summers of 1873 and 1874.[56] Table 3.3 includes all women arrested as madams or brothel inmates during these months. It confirms that madams were more likely to have stable careers than their inmates. Six of the ten women arrested as madams during the summer of 1873 were also arrested in 1874; two had been downwardly mobile and their 1874 arrests were for prostitution, but four continued to hold the status of madam. Even discounting the two downwardly mobile women, the retention rate for madams was 40 percent. In contrast, only twelve of the fifty-three women arrested as inmates in the summer of 1873 were arrested one year later—a retention rate of only 23 percent. Further, this table ignores intracity mobility; many of the inmates still in town after a year may have moved to other firms.

The high turnover among brothel inmates reflected the nature of the market for vice. Where seasonal work patterns affected the size of the male population, as in the cattle towns and mining camps, the supply of prostitutes followed the demand for their services.[57] (In St. Paul, the brothels were said to swell "just before crews of

Table 3.3
Prostitutes and Madams Arrested
during the Summers of 1873 and 1874

	1873	1874	Both
Madams	10[a]	9	4
Prostitutes	53	49[a]	12
Total	63	58	18

[a]Includes two women who were arrested as madams in 1873 and as prostitutes in 1874. They are included in the total for "Both."

lumbermen went into the woods in the autumn and shortly before they returned from the pineries in the spring," as well as when the legislature was in session.)[58] Moreover, the customers' desire for novelty required turnover even when the population was stable. One nineteenth-century madam complained that customers demanded variety: "There are some of the best men in Washington who insists [sic] on having a new girl every time they come. It's a common question, 'Haven't you a new face to show me?' And they want young girls, too—the younger the better. Of course, they get tired of their wives, but I do get out of patience to see that they want a new one every time."[59]

Similarly, Richard Symanski accounts for the high turnover rates in modern Nevada's legal brothels by identifying four functions of turnover: minimizing social friction among the brothel's staff; giving prostitutes a variety of customers and colleagues; supplying customers with a variety of prostitutes; and reducing the risks of a customer becoming emotionally involved with a prostitute.[60] Presumably, most of St. Paul's prostitutes moved on for similar reasons.

Geographic mobility figured into nearly every prostitute's career, but social mobility was less common. The major step within the demimonde was from independent prostitute or brothel inmate to madam, from paying a keeper a portion of one's earnings to collecting from one's "boarders." Obviously, not every prostitute could become a madam, but a substantial number were upwardly mobile. At least thirteen of the forty madams had spent time as an independent prostitute or brothel inmate in St. Paul, and, given the gaps in the inmates' arrest records, the proportion may have been much higher. A better index of opportunities for mobility is that only four of the sixty-one brothel inmates arrested from April to October 1873 went on to manage brothels in St. Paul within the next ten years. Some women may have moved on to run houses in other cities, but it seems reasonable to argue that former inmates would be most likely to open firms in a city with which they were familiar, and particularly in St. Paul, where both the general population and the number of brothels were expanding and the authorities were not repressive. This suggests that perhaps a tenth of all prostitutes were upwardly mobile.[61]

Downward mobility from madam to prostitute was less common, but it did occur. Frank Livingston operated a brothel in St. Paul in 1866. She moved to Minneapolis for a time, then returned to St. Paul, where she had several arrests for visiting a house of ill fame (that is, she was no longer a madam). The *Pioneer* described her: "She has had a hard experience which tells fearfully upon [her] fragile form, and has destroyed that beauty which in former years was her pride and ruin. She is now frequently found in a state of helpless intoxication on our public streets, and makes weekly, and sometimes tri-weekly trips to the police court."[62] At least two other madams stayed in St. Paul and were downwardly mobile, becoming brothel inmates or independent prostitutes.

Leaving Prostitution

The final stage in the deviant career often is hidden because ex-deviants try to divorce themselves from their past to avoid stigma. Sociological studies of deviant careers emphasize the reforming influence of formal social control programs featuring punishment, treatment, or therapeutic interaction with other ex-deviants; little is known about individuals who find their own pathways out of deviance.[63] Yet most nineteenth-century prostitutes left vice voluntarily after a few years; no inmate in St. Paul reported being over thirty. Even if the women lied, reporting themselves younger than their actual ages, they could not hope to remain in prostitution long; each year made them less attractive, less competitive in their marketplace. Finding that the great majority of New York prostitutes were under twenty-five, William Sanger concluded that a typical career led a woman through a series of increasingly disreputable brothels, until she died within a few years. Victorian newspapers embellished this theme; the death of a prostitute contrasted nicely with the surface glitter of her life, offering an obvious moral for the papers' readers.

St. Paul's newspapers gave detailed reports of the deaths of several prostitutes. These accounts suggest the array of risks faced by madams and brothel inmates. Kate Cook, a young inmate, took an abortifacient medicine (against the advice of Kate Hutton, her madam, who encouraged her to have the child) and died of poisoning.[64] Fights and other disorders broke out frequently in the brothels. Although there were no reports of women dying in these incidents, some suffered serious injuries. When Lizzie Caffrey ejected two men from her brothel, one struck her "with a slug shot, knocking her senseless" and nearly killing her.[65] Kate Hutton was shot to death by her lover in an apparent accident; she died in her home rather than her brothel.[66] Suicide attempts were common. Two madams, Hutton and Frankie Brown, tried to poison themselves after being deserted by lovers, and at least five inmates also made suicide attempts, two successfully. Florence Fuller was an inmate in Annie Oleson's brothel when she met and married a customer. Her husband mistreated her, and they separated: "She took in washing, went out at day's labor, and struggled more than any one knew to keep from a life of prostitution." Finally, she returned to the brothel, now managed by Fannie Scheffer, and eventually shot herself.[67]

Prostitution was a hard life, and many women turned to drink or drugs. Drunkenness was an everyday occurrence in the brothels, contributing to the frequent disorders. The testimony at the Robinson arson trial, which offers a glimpse of a typical evening in a brothel, revealed that several of the inmates had been drinking or were drunk.[68] Many prostitutes preferred using morphine or laudanum; they accounted for most of St. Paul's narcotics users. In St. Paul, as elsewhere in late nineteenth-century America, recreational opiate use was closely associated with vice. One druggist, located near several brothels, said: "The customers are all prostitutes, as everybody knows. They are used to the stuff, and take that way of drowning their sorrows or ill feelings. . . . I do not think I have ever sold morphine to a man in St. Paul, and never to a respectable woman."[69] In addition to providing escape, addiction often disrupted the menstrual cycle, thereby serving as a contraceptive.

Alcohol and drugs probably contributed to deaths by natural causes. At least four madams died from disease. Florence Campbell died of heart disease; she had "for years been using whiskey and morphine."[70] Lizzie Caffrey was taken to the hospital to die; her "sinful ways . . . brought her to the verge of the grave and a condition sickening in its details."[71] Sarah Mason's death was due to consumption; Henrietta Charles's death certificate cited "Congestion of the brain" as the cause. All of these women were relatively young; Mason died at twenty-six, Campbell at thirty-one, Caffrey at thirty-four, and Charles at thirty-eight. Kate Hutton was thirty-five when she was shot. Unfortunately, the newspapers were less likely to cover brothel inmates' or independent prostitutes' deaths from disease. The annual reports of the Magdalen Home, however, describe three deaths of prostitutes, including a former inmate of Henrietta Charles's brothel, who entered the Home and found salvation. Obviously, the Home's officers were especially likely to relate tales demonstrating the effectiveness of their good works; there were no reports of deaths of unrepentant women.[72]

Deaths from violence and disease are consistent with Sanger's thesis of inevitable decline, but they are not sufficient proof that most prostitutes died after short careers. The newspapers mentioned eleven deaths of madams or prostitutes, but, as several hundred women must have passed through the city's brothels, far more must have died if Sanger was correct. One method of testing his thesis is to compare brothel inmates with independent prostitutes. Sanger argued that women worked in better brothels when they entered prostitution; as a consequence, brothel inmates should have been younger than other prostitutes. Yet an examination of the arrest ledger's entries for 1873 and 1874 shows no difference in the ages of the two groups. Eleven independent prostitutes were arrested, with a median age of twenty-one (range, eighteen to twenty-seven), compared to twenty-two for brothel inmates. Similarly, five women had one or two arrests for keeping a house of ill fame (suggesting that they operated minor establishments); their median age was twenty-seven (range, eighteen to thirty-five)—the same as the forty madams in midcareer.[73] A further challenge to Sanger's thesis appears in the pattern of inmates' movements between brothels. Although Mary E. Robinson's house ranked above her rivals' brothels, inmates often worked for another firm before joining Robinson.

From April to October 1873, six inmates moved from rival brothels to Robinson's house; two of these women each had worked in at least two other firms before moving to Eighth Street. Contrary to Sanger's claim, prostitutes did not always move down to shabbier establishments.

Furthermore, some prostitutes and madams left vice for respectable or quasi-respectable lives. They retired, got married, or found legitimate work. Their numbers are difficult to estimate because they left few records; most tried to conceal the facts of their past to avoid hostility from respectable citizens, and, once they were no longer "women of the town," the newspapers tended to ignore them. Retirement on one's savings was an option open to the frugal, particularly a madam. Mary E. Robinson's resources were substantial, and Lilly Thompson was said "to have a large number of United States bonds carefully laid away, besides a good sized bank account."[74] If they owned their buildings, madams could turn over the firm to a successor and collect rents; Maggie Morse, Kate Hutton, and Annie Oleson all retired in this fashion.[75]

Marriage probably offered a more common route out of prostitution. Some marriages were unsuccessful, as in Florence Fuller's return to vice and subsequent suicide. Others married and dropped from sight: "a nolle prosequi was entered, as the defendant had left the business, got married, and was respectable."[76] A few prostitutes may have married well. Newspaper stories hinted that prominent men frequented the brothels and sometimes fell in love with the inmates, but the papers were too discreet to publish the details of a marriage between a respectable man and a former madam or prostitute, making it impossible to trace the women once they left vice.

Still other women entered respectability with the aid of reformers. The Home of the Good Shepherd and the Magdalen Home admitted prostitutes as well as other fallen women. The court sentenced some to serve a term in the Home of the Good Shepherd; St. Paul lacked other facilities for incarcerating women during much of this period. Other prostitutes entered the homes because they were pregnant, angry with their lovers, or sincerely interested in reform. The homes' regimen consisted largely of religious instruction and training for domestic service. The Magdalen Home's annual reports contained accounts of successes: prostitutes who found religion and left the home for marriage or respectable employment. Others' experiences ended in failure; they returned to vice.[77] The *Pioneer* mocked one inmate who returned to the brothel: "Black gowns and a quiet respectable life do not possess the charms for the little siren, that pinchbeck jewelry, flashy clothing and panniers do."[78]

Respectable society's refusal to readmit former prostitutes made attempts at reform more difficult. A fallen woman's stigma was not easily shed. After Mary E. Robinson confined herself to legitimate real estate ventures for four years, a newspaper ran two long articles, reminding its readers about her past.[79] Reports from the Magdalen Home spoke of more serious setbacks. One woman left the Home to work as a domestic, but when her employers learned about her past they fired her: "She left the house at 10 o'clock at night, without shelter or friends, after ten months of faithful service and earnest strivings to do right."[80]

Summary

Just as most late-nineteenth-century urban governments adopted policies that tolerated vice, the prostitutes in those cities shared career patterns. Reformers' tracts portrayed vice as a well-coordinated conspiracy: procurers prowled through cities, befriending innocent young women, drugging or tricking them into captivity, and sometimes transporting them great distances to supply the brothels; eventually, the women found themselves trapped under the cruel domination of a madam. In this vision, vice involved a network of exploitative criminals who managed a national, even international, white-slave trade, although case studies of urban vice generally fail to substantiate the existence of these large criminal organizations. The demimonde was organized but, in St. Paul and most other cities, it was a loose organization of colleagues. Madams were independent entrepreneurs who competed with each other for customers, as well as for inmates who might attract these men. The vast majority of prostitutes chose to enter vice, and brothel inmates were free to change houses or leave prostitution altogether.

Like other popular explanations for deviance, the reformers' accounts treated women who entered prostitution as passive—pawns of age, disease, and procurers. In contrast, the sociological concept of the deviant career suggests that prostitutes typically confronted similar problems and chose similar methods of solving them. While prostitutes' careers did not exactly duplicate one another, the women tended to travel along similar pathways. Madams and brothel inmates actively shaped their own careers: they typically entered vice because it offered a higher income and more independence than the other jobs open to them; they sought better opportunities by constantly moving from place to place; some inmates became entrepreneurs, opening their own brothels; and, of those whose fates are known, as many returned to respectability through retirement, marriage, or reform as died at an early age.

In seeking to control their own careers, prostitutes, like respectable men and women, were active participants in the fluid urban scene of the nineteenth century. The city's social structure shaped career paths. For St. Paul's prostitutes, the sexual double standard, the demand for vice, the limited opportunities for respectable work for women, the police department's policy of regulating brothels through regular arrests, and the stigma that followed the women back into respectability provided part of the context within which their careers developed. The individual's choices—to enter or leave vice, to move on to another place, or up or down to another status—took this context into account. Analogous processes shaped respectable careers. Studies of occupational mobility or marriage age assume that individuals' life decisions reflect the social structure, that coherent collective patterns emerge from personal assessments of opportunities and risks. The concept of career offers a framework for such analysis. By examining the impact of changing social structure on career contingencies, historians can better understand the lives of ordinary people, both within and outside deviance.

4

THE CULTURE OF THE BROTHEL

Nineteenth-century reformers described brothel life as a web of exploitative relationships. Their accounts of the pathways into prostitution denied women's responsibility for their deviance; instead, reformers argued that white slavers tricked or forced many young women into vice, while other innocents found themselves condemned to a "life of shame" after being seduced and abandoned by dishonorable men. Similarly, reformers warned that the prostitute, once established in a brothel, found herself at the cruel mercies of madams, pimps, and customers, all bent on further exploitation. In sermons, tracts, and novels, reformers depicted the prostitute's powerlessness before her exploiters. These reformers could not acknowledge the women's independence, their calculated choice of vice as a career. Admitting this would have forced reformers to view prostitutes as independently choosing depravity, challenging the nineteenth-century sexual ideology of female dependence and purity. Reformers needed to see prostitutes as unwilling, innocent victims of exploitation because, as victims, prostitutes deserved rescue, thereby justifying the reformers' good works.

In contrast, modern studies of nineteenth-century vice emphasize prostitutes' independence and solidarity. In part, this interpretation reflects the consensus of labeling theorists and other sociologists that deviants are best understood as rational actors who commit deviant acts in response to their interpretations of their situations. But modern analyses often have an additional, political dimension; their authors present feminist interpretations, emphasizing the historical solidarity of women—even deviant women. Thus, Judith Walkowitz argues that "a strong female subculture was a distinguishing feature of nineteenth-century prostitution."[1] Marion Goldman suggests: "Frontier prostitutes' living and traveling arrangements both reflected and added to their mutual intimacy, and most other aspects of work organization in prostitution also supported solidarity. . . . Prostitutes' isolation from the respectable community created a bond among them, as did their antagonistic economic relationships to customers. They shared a set of customs and an argot which distanced patrons and defined the social reality which they experienced."[2] Finally, Ruth Rosen states: "Despite petty jealousies and competition, the women who lived and worked in the same houses and trade seem to have experienced a continuous bonding."[3] Walkowitz, Goldman, and Rosen qualify these claims, noting that conflict sometimes developed because the women were competitors in the illicit marketplace; nonetheless, all three found strong bonds among the prostitutes they studied.

Once more, the shifting interpretations of nineteenth-century vice become apparent. Where the early reformers saw the brothel as a scene of exploitative horror, some modern scholars seem to find a bastion of female solidarity. But relationships within brothels were rarely one-dimensional. Inside the houses, inmates interacted with one another, as well as with their madams, servants, pimps, and customers. The network of vice also extended outside the brothel; madams and inmates had ties to their buildings' landlords and a variety of business and tradespeople who profited from the marketplace in prostitution. Economics formed the basis for many of these relationships, but friendship, love, jealousy, and other emotions also shaped the links between each prostitute and the rest of the demimonde. This chapter will examine relationships inside St. Paul's illicit marketplace, while the following chapter will consider the ties between vice and the respectable community.

The Brothel's Residents

The madam stood at the center of the brothel's economic and social network. She was a businesswoman, the house's proprietor, and, in some cases, the owner of the building and its lot. She represented her establishment in the courtroom and before the general public. Madams such as Henrietta Charles, Kate Hutton, and Mary E. Robinson were public figures; the newspapers often used the madam's name or nickname to refer to her brothel—"Fort Robinson" or "Swede Annie's house." A particularly notorious madam's name sometimes remained connected to a brothel even after another woman took over the establishment; when Sarah Mason took over Kate Hoffman's house, the brothel continued to be called by the former madam's name.[4] As the brothel's proprietor, the madam had the greatest stake in the business; she stood to make the largest share of the profits. Moreover, under St. Paul's system of regulation, she had the prospect of a stable career; a madam who cooperated with the police to keep her house orderly and paid her fines in the municipal court could reasonably hope to remain in operation for years. An orderly brothel would attract customers without drawing sanctions (other than regular fines) from the authorities. However, keeping a brothel orderly required skill at managing contacts with both the brothel's other residents and those outsiders with ties to vice.

Remarkably little is known about madams' relationships with one another. As colleagues in the illicit marketplace, they appeared in court on the same days, lived in the same districts, and shared many problems. Yet madams' contacts with one another were recorded only when events attracted the newspapers' attention. These tended to be troublesome situations—either disputes between madams or shared threats from the authorities. As brothel proprietors, madams competed with each other in the illicit marketplace. This competition sometimes led to arguments, lawsuits, or assaults. "While taking an oyster stew at the restaurant up town," Henrietta Charles and Kate Hutton "had a ferocious fight, with fists, claws, and whatever they could reach."[5] No reason was given for that fight, but other disputes between madams involved rent payments, jealousy over a lover, and the right to house popular inmates. These disputes usually did not come to public attention unless a madam or some of her inmates raided the competing brothel, perhaps tarring the building or assaulting its occupants.[6]

Just as there are few traces of madams' conflicts with one another, there is little remaining evidence of solidarity among madams. However, reformers' campaigns to eradicate vice by bringing felony charges against madams twice led to reported gestures of solidarity. In 1879, the grand jury indicted several madams. While waiting to hear the charges, Pauline Bell broke down in tears. Kate Hutton "leaned over and gently caressed Pauline, trying to comfort her with the remark: 'Oh, pshaw! Pauline, brace up and put on some style.'"[7] Support could be financial as well as emotional; on another occasion, Mary E. Robinson paid $500 bail for another madam who faced trial in the district court.[8] Crises, then, could cause either conflict or cooperation among madams, but there is no record of the women's relationships under routine, day-to-day circumstances.

Similarly, everyday interaction between madams and inmates rarely attracted the newspapers' notice; the nature of these relationships must be inferred from stories about newsworthy events. Certainly, madams sometimes acted protectively toward their inmates as well as would-be prostitutes. A young woman who asked to join a brothel might be turned away, perhaps because the madam believed she still had a chance to build a respectable life. Madams offered such young women money to pay for their return home or brought them to the attention of the police or clergymen.[9] On the other hand, a madam might help an experienced prostitute join her brothel. When inmate Maud Murdock stabbed a brothel customer, she was jailed until she promised to reform. After her release, Hattie McBride asked the chief of police if Murdock might have permission to join McBride's brothel.[10]

Madams tried to protect their inmates from a range of problems. They paid the inmates' fines at the monthly courtroom appearances and sometimes posted bond or bail when inmates or their pimps faced criminal charges for theft or assault.[11] Madams also advised inmates during personal crises. When Kate Cook became pregnant, her madam, Kate Hutton, encouraged her not to have an abortion.[12] Similarly, Annie Oleson warned Florence Fuller not to marry the customer who later mistreated and abandoned her.[13] These cases came to public notice only because the inmates died—Cook from her abortion, Fuller by suicide; presumably other inmates followed their madams' advice and came to happier ends. After Mary E. Robinson's brothel burned, she told a reporter, "I shall take care of my girls and see that they have enough to eat and to wear also."[14]

These protective acts suggest that madams accepted some responsibility for the welfare of their inmates.

Being the inmate's protector did not necessarily make the madam her friend. Their relationship was not egalitarian; the madam was the inmate's employer and supervisor. Yet madams and inmates occasionally enjoyed recreational activities together—riding a carriage through the streets, drinking in saloons, or dining in restaurants. Mary J. France escorted her inmates to the opera house, where she had reserved prominent seats.[15] These examples suggest that some solidarity could emerge between a madam and her inmates.

On the other hand, madams asserted their authority within their houses. Money often became a focus for disputes between madams and inmates. In a newspaper interview, Maggie Morse explained that she supervised her inmates closely: "As far as receiving money goes, no girl dares to take more than her due, for they all know that if they do, they would be immediately turned out. I can always tell when a girl has more money than she is entitled to."[16] Henrietta Charles called the police when she discovered an inmate and her pimp committing a more serious breach of the brothel's rules—running a badger game inside the house.[17] Some madams took advantage of their control over the money to cheat their inmates: "An unfortunate of more than ordinary attractiveness appeared in the municipal court yesterday afternoon, as prosecuting witness against her landlady, Hattie McBride, a 'cigar dealer' on Robert street. From the story told by Miss Smith it appeared that she had been the principal attraction at the McBride institution, and had earned something over $50 as her share of the profits of the cigar business. The money was absorbed by the somewhat celebrated Hattie, long before it had a chance to cool in the palms of the trusting Smith."[18]

More often, madams accused their inmates of owing money. When an inmate sought to leave a brothel, the madam sometimes refused to release her trunk of belongings until repaid whatever the inmate owed for her board. Under St. Paul's system of regulation, both madams and inmates felt free to carry their disputes to the authorities; they brought charges of theft and other offenses against one another.[19] These disputes revealed some of the tensions inherent in the madam-inmate relationship. If the vicious, exploitative madam featured in white-slave tracts did not exist in St. Paul, neither did the city's madams and inmates achieve the harmonious solidarity implied in modern feminist interpretations of brothel life.

Madams and inmates were not the only brothel workers. The better houses employed servants—perhaps a cook and a chambermaid, as well as a male porter or "wine man." These servants were often black; some lived in the house. In 1870, Mary E. Robinson's brothel held ten inmates and three live-in servants, including one male. (Although several brothels had pianos, there is no record of any employing a "professor" to play music.) Madams sometimes abused their servants; both Henrietta Charles and Kate Hutton—two madams prone to violence—faced charges for beating servants.[20] Most madams also employed men to bring in customers, although Maggie Morse, proprietor of one of the city's finest brothels, noted with pride: "Nearly all of the houses in St. Paul have ropers-in; we have not, and a man was never solicited to visit here."[21] Outside the brothel, other people depended on the vice trade for their living: washerwomen did the brothel's laundry; milliners sewed for prostitutes; and an old woman, Mary Monti, performed the necessary abortions.[22] This constellation of service roles supported prostitution, making the brothels more efficient operations.

Also residing in or near the brothels were the men supported by madams and inmates. These pimps drew the newspapers' special contempt:

> The young man was stylish, after a sort, and sought to wear the airs of a well bred gentleman, somewhat given to "sport." . . His father is represented to be very wealthy, engaged in a lucrative business, and standing among the first business men in [Toledo]. . . . If [his parents] take him home, abandoning without assistance the girl who accompanies him, has supported him in his idleness, and who would evidently undergo any extreme, endurable suffering for him, we may hereafter hear the report of a pistol shot and be able to trace it back to this little piece of life in the low haunts of vice, and the mistreatment of a young girl who is every way the superior of the worthles [sic] vagabond that she has for so long supported.[23]

Surviving records make it impossible to estimate the proportion of prostitutes who had pimps. The men were not subject to St. Paul's system of regular arrests, so they do not appear in the court records. The newspapers preferred to ignore pimps until some noteworthy escapade attracted attention. As a consequence, pimps remain largely hidden from close historical analysis. Two who did achieve notoriety were associated with madams, not inmates, and they drew attention because of the women's notoriety. Ed Wright, a black man with a record of petty crimes, had a long, tempestuous relationship with Kate Hutton. He acknowledged firing the shot that killed her but insisted it was an accident.[24] Hank Clay married Maggie Morse and, according to her, used threats to gain title to some of her property. Eventually, Morse charged him with bigamy and divorced him.[25] In some respects, Wright and Clay resemble other pimps. Like Clay and Morse, pimps and prostitutes often claimed to be, and sometimes were, married. Like Wright, some pimps were involved in crimes, including armed robbery and badger games. The *Pioneer* grouped pimps with other criminals, complaining about the "blacklegs, pimps, thieves, and bruisers" who arrived each spring when the Mississippi opened for navigation.[26] But other pimps held jobs; one worked as a Minneapolis policeman, another in a clothing store.[27] Because so little is known about St. Paul's pimps, it is impossible to say which of these patterns was more common.

Certainly, the relationships between prostitutes and their pimps were complex. On the one hand, they were marked by violence. Pimps were arrested for beating their women; in addition, Wright, Clay, and other madams' pimps sometimes beat inmates and servants. On the other hand, there were gestures of love and support: a prostitute attacking the police officer who tried to arrest her pimp; a pimp bailing out his woman; or a pimp threatening suicide when a prostitute abandoned him. Unfortunately, these glimpses of the prostitute-pimp relationship are too few to support more detailed analysis.[28]

Kinship sometimes linked brothel residents. The newspapers reported at least three cases of inmates who were sisters. Mother-daughter combinations also occurred. Two of Mary J. France's daughters worked in her brothel, and Virginia Paddock, a minor madam, had three inmates in 1870, including her daughters Emily, sixteen, and Matilda, eighteen.[29] Younger children usually were protected from the realities of brothel life; mothers boarded their small children elsewhere, sometimes with Mary Monti, the abortionist.[30] Successful prostitutes could even conceal their profession from their children and other relatives. Kate Bailey, a notorious inmate and later a madam, had her daughter raised in convents in Missouri and Minnesota; years passed before the girl learned her mother's occupation.[31] Similarly, when Henrietta Charles returned to Germany to visit her family, she told them she operated a respectable boarding house. Later, she paid her brother's passage to St. Paul and sent him to a religious college. He was shocked to discover she managed a brothel, but he eventually came to live in the house, "indulging riotously in the wickedness of the establishment. Of course, his ruin has been rapid and sure, so that his present condition is utterly hopeless."[32] Entering prostitution, then, did not inevitably dissolve the women's family ties.

Finally, a brothel might contain an assortment of other people. On April 21, 1870, Cora Webber appeared before the police court and paid fines for herself and three inmates. This routine appearance took a surprising turn; Judge Thomas Howard denounced the system of regulation, levied unusually heavy fines, and threatened to jail any of the assembled madams who continued operating brothels. Two months later, a census enumerator found an unusual group of people in Webber's house: Webber, a prostitute, two female domestics, two male saloon keepers, a housewife married to one of the saloon keepers, and a male laborer. Neither the prostitute nor the servants (who might have been concealing their status as inmates) were among Webber's inmates in April.[33] Perhaps Webber opened her house to respectable lodgers because she was frightened by Judge Howard's threats, but that cannot explain why she acknowledged having a prostitute on the premises. A simpler interpretation is that brothels occasionally housed residents who were not involved in vice.

Brothels, then contained a complicated mixture of people: madams and inmates, perhaps servants and pimps, and, at least occasionally, relatives and lodgers. The web of relationships among these people was tangled. Newspaper stories emphasized conflict within the brothels because reporters considered violent arguments, lawsuits, and other disputes newsworthy. Love, friendship, and supportive behavior made the papers less often, but that may have reflected editors' news judgments more than the absence of solidarity within the demimonde. The relative proportions of conflict and cooperation are not clear, but certainly brothels were scenes of both disruption and solidarity.

Contacts with Respectability

Brothel life was more than the sum of the relationships among the brothel's residents. Those relationships helped shape the ways prostitutes behaved, but the respectable world also had an influence. As long as prostitutes worked in the illicit marketplace, they remained outcasts from respectable society. Because nineteenth-century sexual ideology placed a premium on female virtue, respectable citizens sought to block "fallen women" from entering—and thereby contaminating—respectable society. These moral guardians policed the symbolic borders between vice and virtue. Keeping prostitutes from mixing with respectable people reaffirmed the women's deviant status as well as the moral superiority of "decent people." St. Paul's madams and inmates mocked such respectable pretensions through conspicuous display, a response that infuriated its targets.

Respectable society, in the form of brothel customers, also joined the activities inside the brothel, but on the prostitutes' terms. There is considerable potential for antagonism between prostitutes and their customers; at worst, each views the other with contempt and distrust. In brothels, the women maintained a substantial degree of control over their contacts with customers; they controlled the setting, had the advantage of experience, and could call on other residents for help. They set the terms for the sexual exchange, restrained by the customers' potential for violence and their own desire for repeat business. These themes of display and control offer a basis for understanding the prostitutes' behavior, both off and on the job.

The madams' monthly public appearances in the city's courtroom always drew crowds of spectators who came to see the notorious women fined. The monthly appearances, then, were status degradation ceremonies, occasions for symbolically confirming the deviants' morally tainted characters. However, if respectable people watched to reaffirm their moral superiority over the prostitutes, the women had their revenge. They used the trials as opportunities for conspicuous display. They arrived in "elegantly appointed chariots."[34] Florence Campbell appeared in "gorgeous style. Her white dress fluttered in the breeze like the main sail of the Great Eastern. Her delicate wrists were surrounded by immense gold chain bracelets, while depending from her graceful neck and falling over the front of a heavy black silk basque, was a monstrous gold chain."[35] Henrietta Charles, short and stout, wore a "sky-blue silk and black velvet basque."[36] And Kate Hutton had a collection of expensive costumes to show off her six-foot frame, including a "sea green gown and a black silk roundabout, trimmed all over with pretty little shiny bugles" and a "very rich suit of black velvet."[37]

In part, spending their money on clothing reflected the realities of a migratory life in vice. Most prostitutes were geographically mobile; their possessions had to fit in a trunk. As a consequence, the women bought clothing and jewelry, items they could carry with them. But there also must have been considerable satisfaction in such display. Most women entered prostitution because they could not find respectable work that offered dignity and a reasonable income. Expensive costumes gave proof that the wages of sin were high. Madams could afford very valuable items; Mary E. Robinson owned "a diamond ring set with seven large stones, and a gold cross containing six brilliants of a large size," valued at $1,300.[38] But ordinary inmates also enjoyed conspicuous display:

> From a jaunty black chip hat, adorned with feathers and ribbons, there depended a dotted gauzy veil. . . . A neat green dress with a genteel black sack and neat fitting gloves, with high, brass heeled gaiters completed the toilet of this young lady.[39]

> In a dress of white muslin fluted and frilled, bespangled with bows and gaudy ribbons, high, brass heeled boots, lavender kid gloves, with a high, rakish, brigandish black hat, decorated with flowers and ribbons, jauntily set upon a wilderness of luxuriant curls and friezes. Her face was painted and powdered in an elaborate manner.[40]

The detail with which the newspapers described prostitutes' outfits reveals the effectiveness of such displays. Respectable people were outraged by these demonstrations of material success by women who had violated the fundamental female responsibility to remain pure and subordinate. No wonder that Mayor Edmund Rice responded to antivice reformers by ordering the police to arrest prostitutes who appeared in public "in gaudy or flagrantly striking apparel."[41]

Rice's order was consistent with other official measures to circumscribe prostitutes' behavior. St. Paul's Ordinance No. 10 forbade "any woman of evil name or fame, to ride in any buggy, carriage or other vehicle in the city of St. Paul, or voluntarily walk or appear in company with any person upon the streets of said city, or enter into any saloon, restaurant or eating house."[42] Police made numerous arrests of prostitutes riding in carriages, but the newspapers still found it necessary to remind officers of their duty. After two inmates caused a drunken disturbance on the road to Lake Como, the *Pioneer* complained that prostitutes "go out in large numbers on Sunday and make the woods ring with their drunken, licentious revelry. It is time the offensive conduct was stopped."[43]

These expressions of outrage reveal the importance respectable people placed on segregating vice. To be sure, prostitutes were not arrested every time they appeared on the street; most arrests involved women who were drunk or disorderly in public. But even orderly behavior was forbidden when it intruded too far into the respectable world. Prostitutes could attend performances at the opera house—if they sat in the rear. They could not, however, hide behind masks and mingle with respectable people at masquerade balls. The police explicitly outlined these rules.[44] Such restrictions aimed at maintaining a physical, as well as a symbolic, separation of vice from virtue. Respectable people, backed by the authorities, wanted to exclude prostitution from their lives. When publicly reminded of vice's presence in their city, they responded with outrage. In turn, the flagrant displays by prostitutes provoked more outrage. By dressing colorfully and invading public settings, the women demanded the recognition that the respectable world sought to deny them.

If prostitutes' behavior in public places was constrained, they had greater freedom inside the brothel. Their houses gave madams further opportunities for conspicuous display. During Christmastime, madams hosted housewarming parties, serving wine to guests, including selected members of the respectable community.[45] When Emma Lee held a reception to celebrate reopening her brothel after she spent six months in prison, eight police officers attended in uniform.[46] Forbidden from mixing with respectable people at respectable entertainments, prostitutes responded by inviting guests to their own gatherings.

The luxurious brothel, furnished tastefully at great expense, is part of the myth of Victorian prostitution. Certainly, the furnishings in St. Paul's better brothels were costly. The drawing rooms at Maggie Morse's house were "more elegantly furnished than any private suite of apartments in the city, the velvet carpets, rich furniture, elegant curtains and other accessories, without the piano forte, costing upwards of $1,500."[47] The newspapers pandered to their readers' eagerness to learn about the madams' extravagance. After Mary E. Robinson's brothel burned, both the Pioneer and the Press took the extraordinary step of itemizing $8,961 worth of lost personal property that Robinson was claiming for her insurance. Among other items, the list included:

One velvet stair carpet	$49.00
One marble top center table	22.00
4 Large pictures	40.00
6 Pictures	60.00
1 Bathing tub	104.00
1 Mink fur circular	300.00
Jewelry	100.00
Bedding and table linen	300.00
1 Set silver plated ware	500.00
Gas fixtures	900.00
Wearing apparel	1,000.00
1 Piano	300.00
8 Pictures	60.00
210 yards carpeting	735.00
Wardrobes	350.00
7 Complete sets bedroom furniture	2,236.50
5 sofas, 1 stove, 4 pictures, 2 window shades, 1 walnut stand, 3 spittoons, 1 piece oil cloth, 3 cotton shades, 3 pictures, 8 yards stair carpet, stair brasses, Dutch wool carpet, 2 walnut bedsteads, 2 string beds, 2 hair mattresses, 4 pillows	580.00[48]

At a time when the city's chief of police earned only $1,200 per year, such valuable furnishings served to display the wealth that could be acquired in the illicit marketplace.

Inside the brothel, a variety of nonsexual entertainment was available. Music played; even "cigar stores" had pianos. The "Cave House" once hosted a dance for prostitutes from throughout the city; the party ended in a serious fight, but other, more peaceful gatherings probably went unreported. Mary E. Robinson permitted occasional card games among her customers. But the most important adjunct to the sale of sex was the trade in alcohol. Madams sold beer and wine as a profitable sideline. Customers commonly had a drink or two, often treating the inmates of their choice to drinks as well, before proceeding to the bedroom; further drinking might occur when they returned to the parlor. One customer blamed a brothel disturbance on the madam, who became angry when he sent out for beer rather than buying her wine.[49]

But, of course, brothels existed to sell sex. Sellers of illicit goods and services typically seek control over their customers. Any deviant sale carries the possibility of exploitation or betrayal; the customer might attack or cheat the seller or inform the authorities about the seller's involvement. Sellers usually have more experience with the deviant exchange than their customers, and they face more severe sanctions if caught; therefore, they try to manage the sale transaction. St. Paul's prostitutes controlled the setting of their sexual exchange; within the brothel, they could stage events to insure their customers' cooperation. Maggie Morse explained that a successful brothel required disciplined, coordinated teamwork: "I never retire until all visitors are gone, and I can tell quickly the difference between men who desire to spend money and those who are only looking around. If I see that they do not intend to spend any money, I give the girls a wink and they leave the room. The fellows then soon become tired of me, and they leave, too."[50]

While the madam gave overall direction, individual inmates devised their own methods for attracting the customers' notice. One prostitute with several years' experience found the competition for customers at Kate Hutton's house intense: "being an old stager, she put on a short dress, painted and powdered, and appeared to play the innocent dodge."[51] The brothel's profits depended on successfully manipulating its customers. However much money a man brought to the brothel, the madam and inmates could find ways for him to spend it—drinks and sex cost money, servants and musicians needed tips, and so on. One railroad roustabout reported spending $22.50 during an evening at Henrietta Charles's house, and Mary E. Robinson boasted that her brothel earned $500 per night.[52]

Naturally, nineteenth-century newspapers aimed at the general public avoided explicitly describing sexual activities. Although St. Paul's papers ran hundreds of items about prostitutes, only a handful of these referred to sex. Again, the unusual, rather than the routine, drew the papers' attention. For example, the brothels apparently served some specialized sexual tastes. Some inmates, such as Maud Murdock and the "old stager" described above, dressed as young girls to attract customers. Another brief item mentioned customers "who have achieved eminence as women beaters in houses of prostitution."[53]

The best evidence regarding a typical evening in a brothel comes from the detailed testimony at the Robinson arson trial. Robinson and seven of her inmates testified about the events preceding the fire. According to their testimony, Robinson closed the house on the afternoon of November 16 in order to see an unidentified person off at the railroad station. Customers began arriving around eight o'clock; some thirteen men visited the house that evening. Robinson sold nine pints of wine; some customers brought flasks of whiskey that they mixed with wine. Mary Pierce and a customer who paid to spend the night retired at ten o'clock. By that time, several inmates were feeling the wine's effects. Jennie Bork and Madaline Preston went to bed around eleven. Just before midnight, several customers left "to go to the boat." Five other men remained on the premises, some in the parlor, but at least one upstairs with Pierce, when George Crummey's party arrived. Crummey disrupted this peaceful scene; he demanded wine, argued with Robinson, and started to beat her. Shortly thereafter, the fire began. Presumably, the events preceding Crummey's arrival represented a typical weekday evening in Robinson's relatively refined brothel.[54]

Careers in prostitution involved substantial risks. Customers sometimes beat or robbed the women. Promiscuous sexual contacts led to unwanted pregnancies and venereal disease. And, of course, the threat of arrest and imprisonment remained in the background. Less obvious was the prostitute's contemptible status in the nineteenth-century moral order; the stigma of being fallen, ruined, permanently outside respectability, must have been a serious burden for many women. Prostitutes devised strategies for coping with these risks. Within the brothel, they sought to control the sexual transaction, using the familiar setting, the support of the other women in the house, and their quasi-legitimate status under St. Paul's system of regulation as resources for managing their customers. Outside the brothel, conspicuous display served to shield the women from some of the respectable community's outrage. Control and display, as well as a subculture of solidarity, offered some protection against the risks of prostitution, but they were not always sufficient, as shown by the frequency of alcoholism, drug addiction, and suicide within the demimonde. In their contacts with respectability, some prostitutes paid a heavy price.

Customers and Landlords

Prostitutes bore most of the risks of their trade, but they did not reap all of the benefits. Although most nineteenth-century commentators believed that the prostitute and her customer were equally guilty, they also acknowledged that a double standard existed. The woman's shame was public; she was excluded from respectable society. When a prostitute managed to attend church services or otherwise pass among respectable people, the newspapers expressed shock and outrage. In contrast, the men who frequented brothels were not stigmatized; their respectable reputations were carefully preserved by editors who refused to name them. Aside from the chance of contracting venereal disease, customers shared few of the risks of prostitution.

Just as customers received sexual satisfaction at little risk, another group, composed largely of respectable men, had a safe financial interest in the illicit marketplace. Landlords who owned the buildings used as brothels earned substantial profits—also with little threat to their reputations. Similarly, many business owners, such as proprietors of hotels and night restaurants, believed that brothel customers formed a substantial portion of their trade. Although these landlords and business owners profited from vice, the connection was indirect; they did not view themselves—and were not seen by others—as part of the demimonde. Thus, the web of illicit relationships that began in the brothel extended well into the respectable community, but the stigma of prostitution covered only the brothel's residents.

The newspapers maintained a cloak of discretion around the brothel's customers, adopting several tactics to conceal the men's identities. Most stories about prostitutes simply did not refer to customers. When the story required mentioning a customer, as when a man created a scene in a brothel, the papers printed occupations rather than names. The newspaper stories were most likely to refer to lower-middle-class or working-class customers; railroad roustabouts, soldiers, and traveling salesmen appeared in several stories. In addition to being of modest status, these occupations most likely involved men who lived outside St. Paul. Stories that presumably referred to local residents described the customers in even vaguer terms—"young men" or "roughs," depending on their class. The newspapers rarely gave the customers' names; predictably, most of the exceptions involved visitors to St. Paul. In a fight between two groups of customers that broke out in Mary E. Robinson's house, one group came from outside the city, the other from St. Paul. The newspaper reports identified John Lawrence as the leader of the first group, while discreetly avoiding naming any of the local men. Unless a St. Paul resident provoked the attention of the press, for example, by suing a prostitute for stealing his clothes, his anonymity was nearly assured.[55]

The newspapers playfully admitted that they were being discreet. One article teased about "respectable females who keep houses where large numbers of single men, of good character, and occasionally a few married men, who also have certificates of good moral character, are accommodated with opportunities for 'the pursuit of happiness.'"[56] Such remarks hinted that the press knew more than it was telling, that it had the power knowledge brings, and that it might use that power. When Carrie Morrison explained that a valuable ring in her possession was a gift from a married man, the *Pioneer* smirked: "An interesting question is raised as to who that man is, and how his name would look in print."[57] But these were idle threats; the press routinely named the city's prostitutes but almost never embarrassed the women's customers. Editors denounced the double standard, even as they upheld it.

The double standard was especially apparent when the customers were men of wealth and power. The newspapers noted that such men frequented brothels, mentioning "a prominent ward politician," "one of the city or county officials," and "a well-known merchant" but giving no names.[58] The *Pioneer* hinted that other customers were state officials, describing the city's madams as women "who dress the best and put on more and richer clothing when the Legislature is in session."[59] These teasing references protected the men's anonymity, just as the authorities sometimes arranged matters to avoid embarrassing revelations about elite customers: "On Thursday night a disgraceful disturbance took place . . . at a low house of evil repute, resorted to by colored people and whites promiscuously. It is impossible to obtain the facts of the case as every one that knows anything about them sings mum. It is intimated that two or three 'nice young men' were in the house at the time. They did not appear though yesterday, nor were their names mentioned publicly."[60] Although the police occasionally threatened to expose the respectable men who caused disorders in brothels, they never carried out these threats. Like the newspapers, the authorities walked a fine line, getting whatever advantage they could from their knowledge but never making what they knew public.

Giving too much weight to newspaper items about brothel customers who belonged to St. Paul's elite distorts the analysis of the brothels' clientele. The assumption that many customers were men of considerable wealth and power blends nicely with the myth of the Victorian brothel as an elegant salon. To be sure, the poorest men could not afford to frequent the established brothels, but it was also true that a very wealthy man could afford to keep a mistress. Most brothel customers probably were respectable men who did not belong to the elite. At least four inmates shared this assessment. Mary E. Robinson brought the four from Chicago, but they left after a short stay: "They expressed supreme disgust with the way matters stand here. They say the place isn't aristocratic enough. In Chicago, they say, their companions were the best men in the city—merchants, bankers, capitalists, first class clerks, &c.—men who wear linen shirts and jewelry. Here, they do not find that class of men among the habitués of their boarding houses, but only a low set, who have plenty of money to be sure, but do not sport the ruffled shirts and jewelry of the class above mentioned."[61] The women's complaint is especially noteworthy because Robinson operated the finest brothel in St. Paul at that time.

The arrest ledger offers further confirmation that most customers were neither rich nor powerful. Fifteen men—apparently customers—were arrested for "visiting a house of ill fame."[62] (Of course, other customers may have been arrested on other charges, such as disorderly conduct, resisting arrest, or assault; they cannot be distinguished from noncustomers who were arrested for similar offenses. Nor does the ledger contain the names of influential—or orderly—customers who avoided arrest altogether. Thus, any portrait of brothel customers drawn from the ledger must be incomplete.) All fifteen men reported being single and between twenty-two and twenty-eight. Most held occupations of at least modest status, including two merchants, five farmers, two machinists, and only three laborers. While not conclusive, this suggests that brothels drew the bulk of their customers from the middle ranks of respectable society.

So long as they were orderly, customers rarely risked exposure. But brothel landlords occupied an even safer position; the newspapers never named them or even hinted at their identities. A few of the more successful madams owned their buildings, but most rented their houses. Although Ordinance No. 10 prohibited renting to prostitutes and reformers occasionally urged that landlords be prosecuted, the police never enforced that section of the ordinance. Two arguments justified ignoring the landlords. First, they were not clearly linked to vice; most used buffers to separate themselves from their tenants: "As a matter of course, the owners will not know what base uses their buildings are put to. They always rent through agents. If the agents have rented their buildings to improper parties, the agents will have to assume the responsibility."[63] Second, the *Pioneer Press* worried that sanctioning landlords might be "discriminating in favor of those wealthy courtesans who happen to own the maisons du joie which they occupy."[64]

Although obviously weak, these justifications provided a rationale for not implicating landlords who nonetheless derived substantial profits from vice. In 1881, reformers noted that a madam would pay $1,500 a year to rent a house that might otherwise rent for $300.[65] Such high rents tempted landlords in St. Paul and other cities. In St. Louis and New Orleans, for instance, landlords let brothels invade residential neighborhoods, driving respectable families away. Although the press and the authorities recognized the problem, they rarely held landlords responsible for their part in the illicit marketplace. Prostitutes were deviant; landlords who profited from prostitution were not.

Landlords were not the only respectable figures who benefited from vice. Brothel customers also patronized other establishments. Traveling salesmen and other visitors to the city stayed in hotels and patronized nearby merchants, in addition to visiting the brothels;

even local men ate late dinners in night restaurants. Vice attracted visitors to the city and lubricated the dealings of otherwise respectable firms: "A large percentage of the buying orders of the small town merchant was closed in the saloons or houses of ill fame. This was due to the fact that the small town merchant was snowed in all winter and in the spring when he came to the city to buy his stock of merchandise, he was hungry for a good time."[66] Some merchants believed that salesmen extended their stays in St. Paul because prostitutes were easily available. One estimate had brothel customers bringing St. Paul's hotels an extra $100,000 each year, while other businesses made an additional $50,000. Another estimate put the total extra trade at $60,000 to $70,000 per month.[67] Thus, hotels, night restaurants, and other businesses located near brothels benefited from the illicit marketplace, even though their own operations were treated as though they were completely legitimate. The proprietors of these firms acknowledged their vested interest in continued vice when they spoke in favor of regulation and against prohibition. But, like the landlords, these merchants escaped the condemnation prostitutes received.

Above all, brothels were houses in which women served men. Moralists might denounce both the prostitute and her customer, but, in practice, the woman bore the burden of condemnation. Customers, as well as the landlords and business proprietors who profited from vice, could draw on two important resources—gender and respectability—when they confronted public opinion. Being male shielded them from some criticism. Most people took for granted society's working to males' advantage, and nineteenth-century sexual ideology gave men an excuse: they were compelled by uncontrollable sexual urges to find release. Thus, the female prostitute was weak, fallen, depraved. In contrast, there was something natural and masculine—albeit somewhat amusing—about the male customer. One reporter recalled, "To be known as having a sporting girl stuck on you was quite a feather in one's cap, and to have a landlady 'sweet' on you was almost as proud a distinction as being knighted by one of the kings of Europe."[68] Further, the men benefited from their respectability. The prostitute was already deviant, labeled as an outcast, while her customer had—and retained—a respectable reputation. The newspapers, the police, and the courts accepted these moral rankings; they assigned the blame to the already denigrated women, while virtually ignoring their respectable partners. The women understood this process perfectly; one Washington, D.C., madam complained: "I don't believe there is a woman living who loves the business. Think what it is, never to be free from fear; never to know at what hour of the day or night we may be dragged into the police court, followed by the rabble, hooting at us or calling us vile names, betrayed, insulted, tried, judged, and convicted by the very men who have made us what we are."[69]

Summary

Nineteenth-century prostitutes, like most respectable working- and lower-class women, are relatively inaccessible to historical analysis. Prostitutes almost never left their own written records. And most of what was written about them appeared as distorted atrocity tales in reformers' tracts; outside the major urban centers with their notorious vice districts, few objective reporters tried to describe vice. St. Paul is a partial exception. Its system of regulation made it possible to acknowledge vice publicly; there was no need to pretend prostitution did not exist. The city's newspapers were relatively free to report events in the brothels—reports from which a sketch of brothel life can be developed. Of course, these newspaper stories have some important limitations. Editors published what they deemed newsworthy (thereby making dramatic stories about fights and confrontations more likely), while they refused to print what they thought indecent or irresponsible (thereby concealing most information about sexual activities or the involvement of respectable men as customers or landlords). Still, these stories permit a partial reconstruction of brothel organization and culture.

The web of social relationships that began in the brothel extended into respectable society. The madam and her inmates formed the brothel's core, but they did not exist in an organizational vacuum. The role of prostitute had its reciprocal roles—servant, pimp, customer, landlord, and so on. All of these people were linked to St. Paul's demimonde; in one way or another, they benefited from vice. Yet the city's moral order did not consider them equally culpable. The prostitutes bore the most severe stigma; they were considered depraved, permanently stripped of respectability. According to the prevailing sexual ideology, a woman's virtue, once lost, could not be regained. In contrast, the men who benefited from vice made no permanent sacrifice; pimps could recover their respectability, while customers and landlords never lost it. The people connected with vice experienced very different degrees of condemnation.

The network of relationships linking people in the demimonde was no monolithic criminal conspiracy. Even in those cities where vice enjoyed a partnership with the local political machine, brothels operated as independent businesses. Tom Anderson, the so-called "Mayor of Storyville," was the boss of New Orleans's vice district. He had a financial interest in at least two brothels and owned a few saloons and restaurants in Storyville, but he fell far short of controlling the city's vice. In the Levee, Chicago's vice district where the enterprises were relatively centralized, prostitution trailed gambling and the liquor trade in importance to the machine. All three vice industries paid money to the bosses, but prostitutes could not keep them in office; only the male gamblers and saloon keepers could vote. Moreover, there were advantages of scale in organizing gambling; a central bank could insure individual gamblers against major losses. Prostitution offered no comparable advantage and therefore less motivation for centralizing operations. The reformers' nightmare of a large-scale, organized traffic in women was unfounded; as long as women's opportunities for respectable, well-paid work were constrained, there was no need for a far-flung web of procurers. Although vice sometimes became more tightly organized as the local machine grew in power, prostitution in most nineteenth-century cities could best be characterized as loosely organized.[70]

The relationships between people in this network also had different qualities. Toward an outraged respectable community, prostitutes directed their contempt in the form of conspicuous display. They drew on their experience and used teamwork to control their contacts with customers. And toward one another, prostitutes felt complex, contradictory impulses. Their shared stigma and their constant contact with one another offered a basis for solidarity, as expressed in a variety of supportive gestures. Yet, at bottom, each prostitute was an independent agent; they were competitors in the illicit marketplace. The women had only modest obligations toward their colleagues; they might choose to help one another, but there was a limit to what each might require from the others. These limits were revealed not only in the strife among madams and inmates but in the women's mobility. Solidarity among the women was insufficient to keep prostitutes from drifting from house to house and city to city, in and out of vice.

5

RESPECTABLE RESPONSES
TO REGULATION

St. Paul's system for regulating its brothels was a popular, *public* policy. City officials acknowledged arresting and fining the madams once each month. Far from pretending that they were committed to prohibition, officials defended regulation as the most practical, effective method of controlling vice. Local physicians also supported the system, although they advocated adding compulsory medical inspections to reduce the spread of venereal disease. Even the newspapers sometimes spoke in favor of regulation. In 1867, the *Pioneer* noted that Chicago and St. Louis were considering adopting regulatory systems and suggested, with a touch of civic pride, that "St. Paul was the first city to adopt the license system, and may find it wise also to add [registration and medical inspections]. It is an evil that must be looked in the face, and not handled with kid gloves."[1] Regulation, then, operated in the open, supported by respectable community leaders in government, medicine, and the press.

Although the system enjoyed powerful support, it had its critics. Regulation was vulnerable to criticism from at least three points. First, it violated the popular conception of morality. Critics argued that vice was obviously immoral, that regulation tolerated immorality, and that such toleration was itself immoral. However expedient regulation might be, whatever practical advantages it might offer, the policy was unacceptable because it contradicted fundamental moral principles.

Second, morality aside, regulation violated the spirit of the law. Prostitution was forbidden by both state law and city ordinance, and city officials were sworn to uphold the law, therefore devising and conducting a policy of regulation subverted the law's intent. Critics charged that St. Paul's officials ignored the wishes of the populace (as expressed in its legal codes) and failed to discharge their oaths of office.

Third, regulation was unjust because it discriminated against women. A double standard existed: women were punished, while men were not. In addition to attacking the different treatment of prostitutes and customers, these critics denounced the officials' failure to control St. Paul's other vice industry—gambling. Gamblers operated without interference; aside from infrequent raids, officials made no efforts to eradicate—or even regulate—gambling. Because most gamblers were male, the different treatment of the two vice industries reaffirmed that St. Paul had a double standard of justice. Regulation's critics based their arguments on central values: morality as the basis for policy; the rule of the law; and equal justice.

The system's critics raised important issues that could not be ignored. Respectable citizens honestly disagreed about the best way to control vice. Defenders and critics debated vice policy throughout regulation's operation; the former stressed the need for a practical, effective means of control, while the latter emphasized morality, legality, and fairness. But, as St. Paul grew from a relatively small, relatively new settlement to a larger urban center, regulation became increasingly controversial. Respectable voices, including those of the press, concerned citizens, reformers, and city officials, spoke out more often, trying to affect the course of public policy, and the system of regulation changed in response to shifting attitudes within the respectable community.

Irony and the Press

For St. Paul's newspapers, vice was a staple topic. The local news pages routinely noted the madams' monthly courtroom appearances, in addition to covering deaths, fights, and other newsworthy events in the brothels. Editors adopted a colorful, ironic style to report about vice. They called brothels houses of prostitution, houses of ill fame, bagnios, bawdy houses, sporting houses, temples of vice, domiciles de joie, and "establishments contraband of Ordinance No. 10," among other terms. Similarly, the press used dozens of circumlocutions for prostitutes, including nymphs, social evils, demireps, courtesans, frail sisters, fallen angels, women of the town, soiled doves, strumpets, nymphs du pave, Cyprians, harlots, sporting women, Magdalenes, and scarlet women. Of course, these terms reflect the elaborate language and entertaining style found in many nineteenth-century local news reports. But the existence of multiple synonyms for brothel and prostitute also suggests that vice occupied an important place in the culture of the period. Elaborate vocabularies are one linguistic clue of cultural importance, and the nineteenth-century editor used a large vocabulary to describe prostitution.[2]

Another measure of vice's importance to the press was the amount of space used to cover the demimonde. During the years just after the Civil War, St. Paul's newspapers were four pages long. Most space contained advertising; a typical day's local news might fill a column and a half. Yet editors devoted considerable space to sensational stories about vice. For instance, Mary E. Robinson was the central figure in two trials that received heavy coverage; in 1870, she sued George Crummey for burning her brothel, and in 1872, she was charged with assault and sued for damages by the wife of a prominent attorney. Each trial lasted four days; the *Pioneer* devoted almost seven columns to the first trial and ten columns to the second.[3] Scandal sold newspapers, and circulation was important in a small city with three major daily papers. Of course, each editor denied focusing on scandals, even as he accused his competitors of pandering to their readers. During one such feud, the *Pioneer* labeled the *Dispatch* "the acknowledged and undisputed organ of [the brothels]" and "a receptacle of filth," "indulging in habitual vulgarity, lewd slang, and obscenity." The *Dispatch* retaliated by attacking the "bawdy" morning paper and hinting that the *Pioneer*'s staff attended brothel housewarmings.[4] In fact, both papers observed the same taboos (against describing sexual activity or giving customer's names), while actively covering newsworthy events involving prostitutes.

Editors used irony to avoid taking a stand on the moral and legal issues raised by regulation. Stories about prostitution were laced with amusing phrases: "Mrs. Mary E. Robinson . . . made herself interesting to Judge Malmros at the Police Court, yesterday morning, by depositing with him $67.50, for the use and benefit of the city of St. Paul. Her benefactions are made with such regularity once each month, and are of such a character and size as to cause her to be held high in the estimation of the Christian people of this city."[5] Reporting the story in these terms served several ends: it gave readers the facts about Robinson's appearance while entertaining them; it acknowledged the apparent contradiction between regulation and morality; and it did not take sides in this debate.

The newspapers displayed ambivalence toward regulation. On the one hand, they acknowledged the policy's practical advantages— if vice could not be eradicated, it could at least be controlled. Prostitution had to be "looked in the face." On the other hand, many stories included editorial asides that chided the hypocrisy of tolerating vice: "Such things can't be allowed in St. Paul—not much."[6] These conflicting stances did not represent changes in the editors' attitudes; contradictory comments appeared in news stories throughout regulation's operation. Perhaps editors saw prostitution policy as a minor issue that had the potential to raise passions and carve a serious split in the respectable community. Humor could diffuse this tension; in particular, irony placed distance between the commentator and the issue, implying that the matter should not be taken too seriously. By alternating sides and adopting an ironic posture, editors avoided making enemies over a potentially divisive issue.

Reporters sometimes tempered their irony with cynicism about the realities of vice. In 1873, the *Press* published a lengthy story about a young girl who was tricked into leaving her widowed mother and then, "under the force of circumstances and undue influence, . . . induced to sell her virtue."[7] The *Press* reporter got the story from the YMCA's City Missionary. Two days later, the *Pioneer* gleefully debunked this "sensational Sunday romance."[8] According to its sources in the police department, the woman was an experienced prostitute in her mid-twenties, recently arrived from the vice districts of St. Louis, who had successfully conned both the missionary and the *Press* reporter with her sad tale. Romanticized stories about vice were the exception; most reporters understood the facts of brothel life. Reformers' tracts might portray a world of cruel abductors and desperate escapes from brothels, but the newspapers showed prostitutes who, faced with admittedly unattractive choices, deliberately picked vice. Women's self-serving stories about abduction often merited—and received—cynical examination.

The press, then, followed the lead of others. When reformers attacked vice, the newspapers spoke approvingly of their campaigns, although the stories were quick to declare the battle won. Many news reports concluded by suggesting that the reformers drop vice and adopt a new cause. After one well-publicized reform campaign led to an official report that defended regulation (and represented a defeat for the reformers), the *Pioneer Press* acted as though vice had been eradicated: "Now that the social evil has been set at rest, the subject should be allowed to drop out of the public gaze. Now let the reformer take a whack at the gambling houses and give them a dose of reform."[9] Similarly, when officials defended regulation, the newspapers acknowledged the system's virtues, but they qualified their endorsement by insisting that vice be restrained. When a particular madam attracted attention through disorderly behavior, the newspaper might conclude its story by urging that the police close the house in question.[10] In short, the newspapers took their lead from the news makers.

St. Paul's newspapers provided the principal forum for debating the city's vice policy, but their editors chose to avoid taking sides in this debate. Coverage of respectable people—both regulation's critics and its defenders—was invariably sympathetic; the papers expressed support for each position in turn. But the press continually nudged the debaters toward more moderate positions that might offer a consensus. In the papers' view, reformers should not conduct prolonged campaigns and officials should regulate so as to restrain vice from intruding on respectable life. The artful use of irony further obscured the differences among reformers, officials, and the press. If the press had a clear position, it was that vice policy should not become an issue over which the community split. Otherwise, the newspapers followed rather than led the debate.

Concerned Citizens' Opinions

The newspapers' ambivalence toward St. Paul's vice policy is apparent in the tone of hundreds of news stories. It is far more difficult to assess the attitudes of the city's citizens. Officials, reformers, and, of course, editors had ready access to the papers; in contrast, ordinary people's views rarely saw print. However, citizens confronted vice under three circumstances that help reveal their attitudes about regulation.

First, some people clearly enjoyed the opportunities to observe the monthly courtroom degradation ceremonies. The police court always drew a larger crowd when the madams appeared to pay their fines. Perhaps Durkheim was correct and these observers found social integration in the spectacle of the community's norms being upheld. Some members of the audience may have been curious to see the notorious women; perhaps others found satisfaction in seeing them humbled. These observers' motives remain unknown; only the fact that they watched the trials remains.

The second source of information about citizens' attitudes is more revealing. Madams occasionally faced felony vice charges in the district court, and citizens served on the juries. These trials usually ended in acquittal—surprising verdicts in light of the madams' notoriety. Vice cases were difficult to prove, but the prosecutors and newspapers still criticized jurors for their reluctance to convict. The verdicts suggest that citizens, or at least men (women could not serve on juries), viewed regulation as reasonable; they were unwilling to impose harsher penalties. This is an inference; jurors, like courtroom observers, were not quoted in the press.[11]

To hear citizens express their views, it is necessary to examine the third source of information—citizens' letters published in the newspapers. St. Paul's newspapers did not print many letters to the editor, and relatively few of them discussed vice policy. As might be expected, the published letters displayed a range of opinions and concerns. At one extreme, "Don Quixote" argued for legalizing prostitution: "Moral sewers are as necessary as street sewers. The average young man (not the ideal young man) has three alternatives. That which he adopts if he is a gentleman is to pay for the gratification of his passions."[12] "Don Quixote" was an exception; most letter writers carefully avoided any appearance of condoning vice. When Dr. H. Wedelstaedt swore out a complaint against a brothel in his neighborhood and then failed to appear in court, the *Pioneer* chided him. Wedelstaedt responded with a card explaining that he dropped the charge because the defense attorney promised that the brothel would move. He added that he could hardly be blamed for the continued presence of vice when the city authorities seemed incapable of prohibiting prostitution.[13] In fact, criticizing St. Paul's officials gave a common theme to most of the other letters. This reflects the nature of the letters to newspaper editors; people more often write to criticize than to praise the existing state of affairs. Still, the letter writers found several grounds on which to attack the existing vice policy.

Their most common criticism was that the city's vice policy applied a double standard: it punished women while men went free. Every act of prostitution involved two equally guilty parties, but the customers rarely faced punishment or even exposure: "what is sauce for the goose is *not* sauce for the gander in this case."[14] Letter writers coined new phrases to describe customers—"the frail brotherhood," "he strumpets," and "fallen men"—revealing, in the process, the double standard embedded in the larger culture.[15] Just as the many synonyms for prostitute showed the women's cultural visibility, the lack of widely used, invidious terms for customers exposed the fact that the men were invisible, only rarely noticed or discussed as a problem. Yet, the writers charged, respectable men kept the brothels in business: "Husbands, fathers, brothers and men in high positions, we are told, are prominent supporters of these vile institutions in our city,—liberal patrons of this 'social evil,'—their lavished money adorning in silks and jewelry the shameless women whom they would blush to see in the presence of their wives, daughters and sisters, to whom they are eking out comparatively a mere pittance, though bound by all that is savored in nature, or holy in earth or heaven, to cherish and protect."[16]

Some writers held respectable men responsible for those women who became prostitutes. According to the Magdalen Home's president, many brothel inmates entered vice only after being seduced and betrayed: "They thought they had found a true friend and so believing and trusting they gave the wealth of their life to the man they loved."[17] Thus, men created prostitutes, then kept them in business, yet suffered no disgrace. Why was this double standard maintained? Letter writers argued that men operated the regulatory system for their own benefit. The criminal justice system—from lawmakers through judges, lawyers, and police officers—was an all-male institution: "Men make such laws, men violate them, men execute them—but only on women."[18] Another writer asked why officials punished prostitutes while ignoring gamblers, then answered that the former, as women, could not vote.[19] The double standard, then, could be attacked for several reasons: it ignored men's role in causing women to enter vice; it discriminated against women by punishing prostitutes while leaving their customers alone; and it perpetuated a system, staffed by men, that worked to the advantage of men.

Additionally, some letter writers—particularly those associated with reform campaigns—attacked St. Paul's system of regulation. Not only did the system adopt the double standard, it tolerated immorality. Regulation accepted the continued presence of vice; prohibition was no longer the official goal. The letter writers argued that prostitution could never be condoned; the city's policy was immoral. Worse still, St. Paul profited from the illicit marketplace. The Magdalen Home's president appealed: "Christian women, did you know that the city of St. Paul licenses our sisters at ten dollars a month, payable in advance, to sell their souls and bodies to satan, and if not paid promptly, they are liable to be shut up in the city prison . . . ?"[20] In this view, regulation put the city on the level of pimps and madams by giving officials a vested economic interest in vice. Regulation did not just discriminate against women; it exploited them.

The letter writers suggested a variety of solutions. First, people had to recognize the seriousness of the problem: "May our eyes be open to see our duty, and then do all we can to stay this great flood tide of evil."[21] St. Paul had two institutions, the Home of the Good Shepherd and the Magdalen Home, dedicated to the reform of fallen women. Prostitutes who wanted to quit could find help, although letter writers acknowledged that the ex-prostitute's stigma sometimes kept her from regaining respectability. Respectable people needed to "imitate the Savior" and forgive women trying to reform.[22] At the same time, the letter writers argued that men who frequented brothels should be excluded from respectable society. Customers also needed to reform, and "Christian men" should dedicate themselves to the task, just as respectable women worked with the Magdalen Home's inmates. Other letters pointed to a need for preventive measures. One thought women would not enter vice if they received higher wages for respectable work.[23] Another argued that urban institutions tempted the young, denouncing a new "beer-hall with girls" as a "kindergarten of prostitution" and "a grammar-school of lust."[24] Finally, implicit in most letters was a call for stricter law enforcement, against both prostitutes and customers, aimed at prohibiting vice.[25] The letter writers believed they understood the problem, and their analysis suggested solutions that could help end the social evil.

In summary, the attitudes of ordinary citizens toward vice remain obscured. Among those concerned (and literate) enough to write letters to the editor, there was considerable disenchantment with St. Paul's vice policy. Both the double standard of vice enforcement and the morality of regulation came under attack; the letter writers generally favored tougher measures aimed at prohibiting prostitution. Although such letters appeared infrequently, they reveal a segment of the population that was ready to support reform campaigns. In contrast, the men who served on juries resisted reform. They usually acquitted prostitutes facing felony vice charges, and, as shown below, failure to win felony convictions brought two reform campaigns to a halt. Presumably, the jurors accepted regulation as a reasonable policy. Thus public opinion was divided over vice. There is no way to determine the proportion of citizens on each side of the issue, but both the regulators and the prohibitors could claim some support among the citizenry.

Reformers against Regulation

At least some citizens believed that vice enforcement in general and regulation in particular perpetuated the evils of prostitution. Something had to be done. In efforts to stop regulation, prohibit vice, and restore morality, reformers organized a series of campaigns. Between 1870 and 1883, St. Paul was the scene of five moral crusades against vice and its regulation.[26] These campaigns were mounted by groups of private citizens and a few city officials who found the city's policy morally unacceptable. Resistance to the reformers came from most city officials, the police, and the brothels. The history of these struggles reveals the complex relationships between politics and morality, as well as policing and vice.

Judge Howard Cracks Down (1870)

The first serious threat to regulation came in April 1870, when Judge Thomas Howard, presiding over St. Paul's police court, announced that he would use his powers to drive the brothels out of business. Addressing the madams, in court to hear the monthly charges against them, Howard complained that regulation "has merely resulted in obtaining a revenue for the city, and has not tended to suppress these offensive and flagrant violations of the law. This must be stopped, and I have therefore determined to use all the power the law gives me to either entirely suppress this great evil, or to so far abate and regulate it, that it will be driven from the public streets, and from the places it now occupies with so much shamelessness, so that those who desire to violate the law in this respect will be compelled to go into the byways and hiding places of the city to find these houses."[27] Rather than the customary fine of $25 plus $10 per inmate, Howard ordered each madam to pay $100 plus $25 per inmate and warned that he might imprison offenders who reappeared before his court. The press seemed enthusiastic; the *Pioneer* spoke of Howard's "very laudible [*sic*] attempt" to control vice, and the *Dispatch* said, "Too much credit cannot be given to Judge Howard."[28]

The police responded to Howard's threat to levy higher fines by arresting the madams only on alternate months. There were no arrests in May, but the madams were brought before the police court in June. Of course, arresting the madams once every two months reduced the impact of Howard's heavier fines. In a July court session, Howard argued with Mayor William Lee, Chief of Police Luther Eddy, and Police Captain James King, charging that the police were interfering with his crusade. Howard wanted the police to adopt an aggressive policy and make frequent vice arrests, every day if necessary. Supported by the ranking police officials, the mayor refused to change the policy: "He opposed the heavy fines inflicted upon those poor women. . . . To depart from the established course, and bring up these women oftener than once a month would be too often and amount to a persecution of them. It is impossible to remove the evil. For six thousand years the attempt had been made to eradicate it but the attempt was useless."[29] Lee affirmed the police responsibility to make arrests on properly sworn complaints but indicated that his administration would not support an aggressive policy in which the police constantly swore their own complaints against prostitutes in an effort to close the brothels. Howard needed the support of the police to bring the women before his court; without this support, his crusade was doomed.

The City Council Experiments (1874)

The second attempt at reform had greater impact. At the February 1874 meeting of St. Paul's City Council, Alderman Dowlan offered a resolution "directing that an officer be authorized to watch all the houses of ill fame, and enforce the ordinances, and follow up the matter day after day, and night after night."[30] In the discussion that followed, most members agreed that prostitution should be prohibited. Various strategies were considered, including arresting prostitutes' customers and publishing their names, and closing the houses located downtown. However, Alderman Richter defended regulation and warned: "Drive those houses into the outskirts and you will have robberies and murders every night. Why? Because the houses will be outside of the control of the police."[31] But when it came to a vote, Dowlan's resolution passed, and St. Paul began a brief experiment with a policy of prohibition.

The new system was scheduled to begin on March 1. As the date approached, the newspapers reported that many prostitutes were leaving town and that madams were either closing their brothels or converting them into respectable boardinghouses. Mary E. Robinson, the city's most notorious madam, announced her retirement and placed her brothel's furnishings up for auction.[32] But other news reports warned that prohibition would fail. The special policeman would be bribed and "the 'evil' . . . will distribute itself throughout the city under various flimsy disguises. The next question is 'How is morality to attack it in this last shape?' 'and will not the old system in the end prove the better of the two?' It is quite evident that the closing process is not destined to extinguish or abate the evil to any remarkable extent."[33]

The skeptics proved correct. On March 10, Lou Adams was arrested and charged with keeping a house of ill fame. She requested a jury trial—the first test of the new system. Adams acknowledged that she had kept a brothel under the old system of regulation but claimed that the women in her house were now working as dressmakers. In the face of this unlikely testimony, the jury acquitted her. Two days later, the authorities tried again, arresting two women for visiting Adams's house for purposes of prostitution. The eight-man jury voted six to two in favor of acquitting the "dressmakers." The *Pioneer* complained that the juries' standards for proof "require every fact to be riveted and double bolted through and through, before a jury can be convinced, and even the jury will keep its eyes very wide open for some little crack or crevice through which the prisoner can be let out." The next day, Adams and her two inmates were back before the court, but the charges against them were dismissed.[34] Without the cooperation of the citizens on juries, the new system failed its test.

In its March 20 meeting, the city council considered a new resolution that would reinstate the regulatory system. Alderman Richter argued "that the only result of the trials of the women arrested had been that they had made the City Council the laughing stock of the city. He charged further than [sic] an officer had been taken off of a beat where there were thousands of dollars worth of property that needed protection and placed to watch the house on Nash street."[35] The resolution was sent to a special committee for further study. In June, amid complaints of increased activity by streetwalkers, St. Paul resumed its policy of regulation. Vice had not been prohibited; Mary E. Robinson had retired, but the other five major brothels were still in operation.[36] The 1874 experiment with prohibition lasted only three months.

Reverend McKibbin's Crusade (1878–80)

The third attack on regulation was led by Reverend William McKibbin, the pastor of Central Presbyterian Church. McKibbin began with a January 11, 1878, letter to the *Pioneer Press* entitled "Have We in This City a Licensed System of Prostitution?" He pointed out that, while the state and city statutes were intended to prohibit vice, St. Paul's system of regulation fell far short of the lawmakers' goal. Regulation made "the community a virtual stockholder in these infamous institutions, increasing its revenues with their prosperity, and filling its treasury with money paid for the privilege of ensnaring the ignorant and the young, and waging war upon the holiest affections and highest interests of society."[37] McKibbin organized some of the city's "most prominent citizens" into a crusading organization, later formally named the Society for the Suppression of Vice. They asked to present their case before the city council. As the meeting approached, the newspapers ran several stories, detailing the scope of vice in St. Paul and speculating about possible tactics to achieve prohibition.[38]

Before the council, McKibbin and Thomas Cochran, a real estate broker, described the system of regulation, pointed to its moral and legal shortcomings, and declared their organization's determination to prohibit vice. They reported that the mayor, James Maxfield, had agreed to follow whatever policy toward vice the council recommended. In response, the council appointed a committee to investigate policy options and make a recommendation. The committee held several meetings with reform leaders, local physicians, and city officials. Its report, made on March 5, 1878, generally affirmed the existing policy of regulation. The report began by recasting the terms for the debate, identifying two opposing directions for reform: formally licensing the brothels and requiring medical inspections; or "what is known as the raiding, harassing, or stamping out system."[39] It proceeded to chart a middle course between these extremes by ranking four forms of prostitution in order of their dangers to the community: "cigar stores" were considered most "mischievous," then "sewing girls" operating from private furnished rooms, brothels on well-traveled streets, and, finally, brothels on the less frequented streets. It recommended that "the first duty of the city is to remove temptation from the innocent and unwary, and to this end . . . all prostitution existing under the head of other callings [should] be, as soon and so far as possible, summarily suppressed. . . . All houses of prostitution upon the more public and traveled thoroughfares . . . should be suppressed as speedily as possible, and under no circumstances should another house of prostitution be allowed to be opened in the city."[40] By emphasizing the prohibition of nonbrothel prostitution, the committee ignored McKibbin's criticism that regulation made the city a partner in the vice industry. Later that spring, the city council did consider a plan to contribute the money collected from the madams' fines to charities dedicated to the reform of fallen women, but the proposal failed to pass.[41]

In response to the committee's report, Chief of Police James King ordered his officers to prohibit prostitution in "cigar stores" and private rooming houses. The *Pioneer Press* declared: "That settles the business—the evil will now be banished from our midst and the missionaries can sleep in peace."[42] This exaggerated the reform's impact. Eight major brothels remained open throughout 1878, although a ninth house closed when its madam, Lizzie Caffrey, died.[43]

McKibbin's reformers would not give up. In 1879, they turned to seeking felony indictments from the grand jury. Under Minnesota law, the district court could sentence convicted madams to one year in prison, and the reformers hoped the threat of imprisonment would drive the houses out of business. With several reformers among its members, the grand jury heard testimony about the extent of vice in St. Paul. (One planned witness did not appear. The reformers hired a Chicago detective to gather evidence for their case, but he was spotted on his first visit to Mary J. France's brothel, where an inmate assured him that the women in the house were respectably employed: "Why, sir; I sew for a living, another sings, another paints, another gives music lessons."[44]) But other witnesses, including the reformers' new president, customs inspector W. L. Wilson, convinced the jurors that the brothels were scenes of prostitution. In May 1879, the grand jury issued indictments against seven madams, along with a report criticizing the policy of regulation and arguing that brothels damaged property values.

Of the women charged, only Maggie Morse pled guilty. Judge Westcott Wilkin disappointed the reformers by fining Morse $300 rather than sentencing her to prison. He explained that it was her first appearance before the district court and that, having regularly paid fines in the municipal court, she "regarded herself as being protected from any other punishment."[45] The six remaining madams pled not guilty and added an accompanying plea that, since they had already been convicted and punished in municipal court for keeping brothels, the grand jury indictments were illegitimate. Wilkin disappointed the reformers again by accepting this argument, and the prosecutor began appealing Wilkin's ruling to the state supreme court. But rather than wait for the higher court's ruling, the reformers sought new indictments from the grand jury. The new indictments were issued on the afternoon of October 12—just hours after the madams were brought suddenly before the municipal court, apparently after being warned about the indictments. Defense attorneys assured reporters that the timing was coincidental, but the maneuver left the reformers open to new charges of double jeopardy. The new indictments were not pursued.[46]

Finally, in June 1880, the Minnesota Supreme Court ruled that the grand jury indictments were legitimate.[47] McKibbin had already left St. Paul for a congregation in Pittsburgh, but the madams remained in the city. They appeared in district court, where Judge

Wilkin fined them $150 per indictment and warned that they could no longer expect clemency in felony cases. Once more, the *Pioneer Press* heralded a new era: "It can now be considered settled that St. Paul is to have no more houses of prostitution."[48] But less than two weeks later, the same paper printed a short item: "The mesdames who manage the houses of ill-fame were hauled up as usual . . . to make their regular contributions to the exchequer of the city."[49] After thirty months, the reformers had won their battle, but they were apparently too exhausted and, without McKibbin's leadership, too disorganized to pursue the further indictments needed to win the war. At the 1881 ceremony inaugurating the new city officers, both the outgoing mayor, William Dawson, and his successor, Edmund Rice, spoke in favor of regulation and criticized reform efforts as impractical. The reformers' only response was an angry letter from Thomas Cochran to the *Pioneer Press*, emphasizing that regulation was inconsistent with morality.[50]

Protecting Irvine Park (1881)

The fourth attack on regulation reflected economic interests rather than moral conviction. Increasingly, St. Paul's brothels, gambling "hells," and disreputable saloons were concentrated "under the hill." This vice district stood between downtown and the respectable residential neighborhood growing around Irvine Park, southwest of the city. In July 1881, a committee of respectable property holders, reportedly owning over $400,000 worth of real estate in the area, campaigned to rid their district of vice. The committee, which included at least three lawyers, emphasized that they were not trying to prohibit prostitution in St. Paul; they just wanted the houses driven away from their neighborhood. The committee received no satisfaction; the district had long associations with vice, and officials probably preferred the status quo to the conflicts sure to arise if they tried to move the brothels into another district. When the city government failed to respond to its campaign, the Irvine Park committee turned to the grand jury for another investigation of vice. In October 1881, thirteen madams were indicted.[51]

The new trials got off to a promising start when juries quickly convicted Emma Lee and Nellie Otis. The next three trials went less well: Carrie McCarthy's trial ended in a hung jury; Kitty Smith was convicted, but only after lengthy deliberations; and Kitty France was

acquitted. The prosecutor began the next case, against Ray Lawrence, but gave up in the middle of the trial, complaining that widespread resistance to the prosecutions made further trials impossible.[52] When issuing its indictments, the grand jury had complained
about "the ostensible ignorance of some of the police force of what
the public supposes them to be fully familiar with, and which from
the nature of their duties they should be."[53] Now the prosecutor reported that many citizens refused to sit on juries in the madams'
cases and that

> there seems to have been some unseen influence at work to dissolve
> and emasculate the testimony. Unseen and unexpected impedi-
> ments were found in his way. Testimony that was strong before the
> court opened, and in the grand jury, lost its point on the way to
> court. Witnesses disappeared and a general dissipation of testimony
> has been visible. As the trials have progressed there can be no ques-
> tion the feeling of sympathy has increased to real opposition to con-
> viction, and juries . . . have almost required demonstration of guilt
> so absolutely conclusive that a trial by jury was almost nullified.[54]

The prosecutor dropped the remaining cases.

The Irvine Park property holders' campaign had some impact.
The three convicted madams appealed. Eventually, the Minnesota
Supreme Court upheld their convictions, and Emma Lee, the only
one of the three still in St. Paul, served six months in prison. Most
of the other brothels remained open, but the madams were not sub-
jected to monthly arrests while the city waited for the Supreme
Court's decision. Once the verdicts were upheld, Mayor Rice formally announced that regulation would resume and, in January
1883, the madams returned to the municipal court.[55]

Mayor O'Brien's Policy (1883–85)

The fifth attack on regulation was led by Christopher O'Brien, St.
Paul's mayor from 1883 to 1885. O'Brien ran for office with the support of reform leaders; Thomas Cochran nominated him at the Republican convention. He also received the Democratic nomination
and was elected without opposition after a quiet campaign. His first
actions as mayor, however, were controversial; he announced that
he would strictly enforce the city ordinances dealing with liquor,
gambling, and prostitution. O'Brien ordered the brothels closed and

gave the inmates three days to leave town. Under the new policy, police prevented men from entering known houses of prostitution and raided the new brothels that sprang up as prostitutes moved to avoid arrest. Arrested prostitutes who refused to plead guilty to violating the city ordinance found themselves facing felony vice charges and those convicted on felony charges received jail sentences. Under O'Brien's leadership, the city mounted a serious campaign to suppress vice. When a man came to St. Paul in search of his wife, who had apparently run off to become a prostitute, the *Pioneer Press* could report: "He was referred to Minneapolis, as there were no regular houses of ill-fame in St. Paul."[56]

But O'Brien's campaign met stiff resistance; some citizens preferred a policy of regulation. During one trial following a police raid, the jury interrupted its deliberations and "asked the court if they would be justified in rendering a verdict of guilty, while they considered the principle of the prosecution unjust."[57] More important, some merchants objected to the new policy. Owners of night restaurants, hotels, and "under the hill" businesses complained of substantial losses; they argued that prohibition drove away traveling salesmen as well as residents of outlying communities who came to St. Paul to trade. These visitors expected to combine their business trips with pleasure and, in the face of O'Brien's reforms, they went instead to Minneapolis, where more liberal vice policies prevailed. In addition, merchants for whom prostitutes constituted a substantial portion of their clientele complained of losses. The city council debated O'Brien's policy only two months after it took effect. Opponents of reform charged that, in addition to damaging trade, prohibition had scattered prostitutes throughout the city to work out of private rooms or as streetwalkers, increased the incidence of venereal disease by making the women afraid to consult physicians, and corrupted young men who "would blush to be seen entering such a house, but were readily drawn into rooms."[58]

O'Brien, Cochran, and other reformers answered these charges. In a lengthy interview, O'Brien attacked the unprincipled position taken by his critics: "One whose moral nature is so constituted that he can openly advocate the necessity of the indulgence and practice of any vice, is not in a position to be listened to by any person who has either been taught or believes common principles of decency and morality." He went on to detail the evils of regulated vice: "It can be very readily shown that nine-tenths of the crime originating and committed in this city originated in and were perpetuated because of the license system that had been established. The names could be given of at least 100, and perhaps more, of our young men who have been utterly and irretrievably ruined by reason of their indulgence."[59] Further, regulation encouraged the police to treat vice as a quasi-legitimate business rather than an illicit enterprise; eight officers dressed in full uniform had attended Emma Lee's reception to mark her release from prison and the reopening of her brothel. Several of O'Brien's supporters joined to refute the critics' other charges. They argued that prohibition was effective: there was no evidence of widespread activity by streetwalkers or roomers, and venereal disease did not appear to be increasing. Opponents' efforts to reestablish regulation through the city council failed; O'Brien's reform remained in effect throughout his two years in office.

O'Brien did not run for reelection in 1885, but vice policy became a central issue in the campaign.[60] The Democrats nominated Edmund Rice, the popular former mayor. The Republican *Pioneer Press* viewed Rice's candidacy as a front for a coalition of corrupt politicians and the vice interests; its Election Day issue warned that gamblers and saloon keepers had contributed heavily to the Democrats, that "imported thugs and thieves and blacklegs" planned to intimidate voters, and that the police might fail to act because some officers were corrupt and supported the return to an open vice policy.[61] Rice won the election, receiving 62.1 percent of the vote citywide, and 70.6 percent in the election districts that had contained regulated brothels before O'Brien took office. The *Pioneer Press* attributed the result to a well-organized campaign by machine politicians and saloon keepers to get out the vote and added: "The nameless thing was an element in this contest, and the flutter of the scarlet garments determined many a vote"; it foresaw an administration in which criminals of all sorts "could ply their varied villainies with only enough molestation to keep up appearances."[62]

The partisan rhetoric exaggerated the debate's emotional pitch; Rice's decision to reinstate a policy of regulation for the brothels did not meet loud opposition. Under O'Brien, the madams did not pay regular fines, but neither did prostitution disappear. Police struggled to keep the town "closed" and arrest the prostitutes who operated from secret brothels, private rooms, and street corners. This experience with prohibition made regulation's advantages more apparent. In his inaugural address, Rice declared: "If it were possible and wise for mortals to reconstruct human nature as respects this or all other known evils, it of course might be extinguished; but as that cannot be, and considering that it is prominently in our midst and staring us in the face, we must treat it as a practical question and deal with it like other evils incident to large cities, by police and sanitary control."[63] Even the *Pioneer Press* editorial writer approved: "After the lessons of recent experiences, the most moral will not be disposed to quarrel with what may be called the quarantine policy enunciated by Mr. Rice."[64] Madams were once more brought before the municipal court on a regular basis. During 1885, the familiar names of Pauline Bell, Ray Lawrence, Emma Lee, and Alice Percy reappeared in the court docket, charged with keeping houses of ill fame. All had been madams before O'Brien's election and presumably they had managed to operate their brothels throughout his term of office.[65] Thus, even the fifth and most successful reform campaign failed to permanently disrupt St. Paul's illicit marketplace for vice. Regulation remained in effect (and presumably under attack) for several more years. However, this analysis ends with O'Brien's reforms because, by driving vice underground for two years, the policies created a gap in the court records, making it nearly impossible to trace individual madams and prostitutes.

Summary

Regulation was a controversial policy, yet all five moral crusades against the system eventually failed. In 1870, Judge Howard tried to force the brothels out of business but found the police unwilling to cooperate. Four years later, the city council's experiment with prohibition ended after only three months. Reverend McKibbin and the Society for the Prevention of Vice announced their determination to close the brothels in early 1878, but by the time the court cases they instigated were finally settled in 1880, the reformers were disorganized and discouraged. The felony cases instituted by the Irvine Park property holders, begun in 1881 and concluded in late 1882, led to one madam's imprisonment, but the rest of the brothels "under the hill" remained in business. Finally, Mayor O'Brien's "closed town" reopened as soon as his successor took office. Regulation's opponents were prominent figures: a police court judge, city councilmen, ministers and businessmen, property holders, and a mayor. Why were their attacks ineffective? Why was regulation such a durable policy?

One explanation might emphasize the economic interests that powerful individuals or groups had in continuing regulation. To be sure, some merchants whose businesses profited from the brothels and their customers protested against O'Brien's reforms. The city government also had a vested interest in regulation because the madams' fines accounted for a substantial proportion of its lower court's modest revenues. Still others profited by renting their buildings to madams for considerably larger sums than they could demand from respectable tenants.

While these merchants, officials, and property holders had a stake in continuing regulation, the scope of their interests should not be exaggerated. The merchants were not powerful enough to change O'Brien's policies; the fines collected in the lower court accounted for only a small proportion of all city income; and, while some madams rented from respectable landlords, others owned their buildings or rented from women who were or had been madams. Overall, the economic interests in regulation seem limited. Moreover, the Irvine Park property holders' crusade demonstrated that other prominent citizens had an economic interest in prohibiting at least those brothels near their holdings. It is not clear that those who profited from regulation outnumbered or held more powerful positions than those who felt that regulation cost them money.

The debate over regulation in St. Paul is better characterized as a struggle between morality and control. Most of the reformers who mounted crusades against regulation, including Judge Howard, Reverend McKibbin, Alderman Dowlan, and Mayor O'Brien, objected to the system on moral grounds. Their attack was a principled one: St. Paul should not tolerate vice under any circumstances; the city should strive to prohibit prostitution. They did not argue that regulation exacerbated the evils of prostitution or that St. Paul's brothels were especially evil, harboring more than their share of diseased prostitutes or forcing young women into vice. Rather, the prohibitionists objected to regulation because, through regular arrests, the city seemed to legitimize an immoral industry. Vice was vice, whatever its particulars, and it demanded prohibition. The way the madams ran their businesses was not relevant; any brothel, no matter how orderly or discreet, was morally objectionable.

For regulation's defenders—a group that included most city officials and police officers—a practical concern about social order was of central importance. Their goal was to maintain order, and they repeatedly defended regulation because it gave them a measure of control over the disorderly world of vice. The regulators based their arguments on a central proposition: prostitutes could not be prohibited. Therefore, the city should bow to the inevitable and, rather than futilely try to prohibit vice, develop practical methods to control it. The system of monthly arrests served this purpose, giving the police the power to close disorderly brothels while letting cooperative madams stay in business. Under this system, vice was a quasi-legitimate industry. This was an ill-defined status; as the prohibitionists noted, regulation ignored the intent of the state laws and city ordinances governing vice. The system depended upon the knowing cooperation of practical men—women might work to reform prostitutes, but regulation was men's work—who understood the need for control. For regulation's defenders, morality was irrelevant.

Most citizens apparently sided with the regulators. The prohibitionists never tried to rally large numbers to their cause. They felt that decency demanded that they be discreet; public debates over vice policy threatened to become offensive. Although some letters to the editor attacked regulation, the men who sat on juries proved reluctant to convict madams on felony charges. The facts of the cases could not have been at issue; every newspaper reader knew the names of the city's madams. Rather, the jurors sympathized with the women, viewing their prosecution as unfair. The madams were businesswomen who supplied a service; moreover, they had paid the taxes the city demanded. Further prosecution and threats of imprisonment seemed unfair. The citizens, like the newspapers, were ambivalent: they saw prostitution as illicit but inevitable, an evil that had to be accommodated and, they hoped, controlled.

Officials and the general public supported regulation, but the police played the key role. Even the prohibitionists sought to use the law and the police to close the brothels and restore morality. Because everyone acknowledged that the police were the appropriate agents for dealing with prostitution, police concerns shaped vice policy. The police wanted to maintain order, and, since regulation offered a means of gaining the madams' cooperation in keeping order, officers fought to preserve the system. On the other hand, the police had no responsibility for controlling venereal disease. Although physicians repeatedly urged that St. Paul make medical inspections part of the regulatory system, their advice was ignored. St. Paul's policy toward vice reveals the importance of social control agents in shaping the policies they carry out.

6

OFFICIALS AND THE DECLINE
OF REGULATION

Social control policies have consequences; they affect deviants, social control agents, and the surrounding community. The choice of one control strategy over another may alter the incidence of deviant acts, the demand for social control agents' services, people's perceptions of their community as a safe or dangerous place, as well as dozens of other contingencies. Sociologists know relatively little about these effects because, rather than exploring different strategies, most studies simply assume that social control agents pursue policies of prohibition. St. Paul's system for regulating brothels offers a useful case for comparison, revealing some of regulation's consequences.

For St. Paul's police, improved social order was the most important consequence of regulation. The system let them supervise the illicit marketplace and gave them the power to reward cooperative—and punish recalcitrant—madams. Madams who kept their brothels orderly and called the police when trouble started were allowed to remain in business, while the police closed houses that were scenes of white slavery or excessive violence or theft. By permitting orderly brothel prostitution, the police could crack down on flagrant streetwalking; independent prostitutes who were arrested received relatively severe penalties. The brothels always had their share of trouble, but regulation minimized these problems by giving the police access to the demimonde. Police officers tried to divert reformers and preserve regulation because they believed that the system maximized their control and reduced the disorder associated with vice.

Madams and brothel inmates benefited from regulation in a related manner: they gained a sense of stability. When social control agents adopt prohibition as their goal, deviants must act secretly to protect their operations from disruption. They can never be sure whether they will be discovered and sanctioned by the agents. But in St. Paul, madams could be reasonably confident that their brothels would be left alone so long as they paid their fines and cooperated with the authorities in maintaining order. Some houses remained in operation for years, their madams earning enough to retire. Even the inmates, who rarely stayed for long, were relatively secure. If they behaved themselves, they never received sanctions more severe than regular fines (customarily paid by the madam). Stabilizing the illicit marketplace fostered ties of solidarity among madams and inmates; within limits, they could call upon one another for help. Prostitution remained a hard life, but regulation made careers in vice relatively stable.[1]

Regulation also served the interests of brothel customers. It assured that an illicit marketplace was available in a known location, to meet their demands for sexual services. Further, regulation preserved the customers' safety. Customers paid high prices and sometimes spent all the money they brought to the brothels, but they ran lower risks of being cheated, assaulted, or robbed because St. Paul's police insisted that the houses be reasonably orderly. This protection extended to the customers' reputations. So long as they behaved in an orderly manner, customers risked neither arrest by the police nor exposure by the press. To be sure, the enforcement of prostitution laws rarely punishes customers regardless of the social control agents' strategy. But in St. Paul, customers ran no greater risks than in cities with other vice policies, and, in some respects, such as the reduced danger of violence or theft, they were probably better off.

Unlike many social control tactics that tolerate deviance, regulation in St. Paul was visible; the newspapers and city officials openly explained the system and ordinary citizens understood its operation. This visibility, in turn, had consequences. It reduced opportunities for police corruption. When social control agencies seek to prohibit illicit marketplaces, corruption often emerges as a major problem. Agents must keep their investigations secret if they are to infiltrate the underground marketplace, but this secrecy provides a cloak for bribery, malfeasance, and other deviance by officials. In contrast, St. Paul's police had relatively little leverage on the city's prostitutes because enforcement took place in the open; officers had fewer favors they could offer the women, and fewer threats they could make. If bribery existed, the paucity of accusations (or even hints) about corruption suggests it occurred on a modest scale. On the other hand, regulation's visibility caused political conflict in St. Paul's community. Because the authorities made no secret of their regulatory policy, the system periodically came under attack by citizens who found it offensive. The reformers' moral crusades were as much a consequence of regulation's visibility as was limited police corruption.

Of course, regulation could not solve all of the problems associated with vice. In particular, St. Paul's system lacked provisions for compulsory medical inspections, which might have reduced the spread of venereal disease. Local physicians favored medical registration and inspections, but the authorities never added these measures to the system. Of course, regulation's visibility may have made prostitutes more willing to have voluntary examinations, but there is no way to know if this occurred.

St. Paul's system of regulation, then, gave the police control over vice, stabilized the prostitutes' workplace, protected the brothels' customers from injury or disgrace, and exposed social control activities to the public. For all these reasons, city officials defended the policy. However, regulation's day was ending. The Progressive movement mounted the next campaign against tolerating vice, and this time the reformers won an enduring victory—of sorts—in St. Paul and most other American cities.

St. Paul's Officials and Vice Policy

As officials who launched antivice campaigns, Judge Howard, Alderman Dowlan, and Mayor O'Brien were exceptions; most St. Paul

officials in the decades following the Civil War defended the system
of regulating brothels through arrests. These regulators gave a standard justification for the policy. They began by adopting William
Sanger's argument that prostitution was inevitable: history showed
that every society had prostitutes; all attempts to prohibit vice had
failed. To be sure, prostitution could not simply be ignored; left
alone, "it spreads itself in all directions where it can gain a footing,
disseminating disease and pollution among the unguarded youth of
both sexes, tainting their souls, poisoning their bodies and entailing
upon their descendants . . . frightful and ineradicable maladies."[2]
Yet overly aggressive policies aimed at prohibition produced equally
damaging results: hiding from the threat of severe sanctions, prostitutes would spread throughout the city; without supervision, they
would rob customers, spread disease, and entrap the innocent.

Regulation offered a middle path, a practical way of avoiding the
problems posed by both laissez faire and aggressive enforcement.
Asked by a grand juror about streetwalking in St. Paul, police detective John Bresett replied: "There is some, but not half nor a quarter
as much as there would be if the regular houses were broken up.
Then it would be forced into nooks and corners. There is no doubt
the best way is to manage to cage the evil up in some location in the
city where it would least disturb people and where the legal authorities could exercise a controlling influence over it."[3] Reformers denounced regulation as tolerating immorality, but St. Paul's officials
countered that, by giving the police a practical method of controlling vice, regulation offered morality its best protection.

Just as the officials designed their rationale to neutralize the prohibitionists' moral objections, they interpreted the law in a manner
consistent with regulation. Reformers complained that regulation
violated the intent of state and local statutes aimed at prohibiting
vice. In response, officials emphasized that regulatory actions were
legal, and they questioned the legality of reformers' proposals. For
instance, officials carefully distinguished between regulation and licensed prostitution. They insisted they had no legal power to (and
did not) license illicit enterprises; instead, the system of regulation
involved their legal powers to arrest and sanction offenders. To be
sure, most acts of prostitution did not lead to arrests, but that reflected the paucity of sworn complaints by citizens against the
brothels. Whenever a citizen swore a complaint, the police made an

arrest. Critics who demanded that the police make more arrests on their own initiative were unreasonable; the police had other duties and could not devote all their time to controlling vice.

Officials also warned that aggressive law enforcement might invite abuses of police power. When Judge Howard urged that the police make daily vice arrests, Mayor Lee warned against placing "these unfortunate women . . . entirely at the mercy of . . . the police force."[4] Similarly, ranking police officers carefully instructed their men to observe the law when making vice arrests; this not only helped restrain potential abuses by officers but also let officials invoke legal constraints to explain the continued presence of prostitution. Police could only make arrests on the basis of sworn complaints, officers' direct observation of illegal acts, and so on.[5] Officials used these constraints to resist cooperating with reform campaigns, frustrating reformers who found it difficult to get police to make arrests and juries to find madams guilty of felonies. On still other occasions, police officers hindered efforts to obtain felony vice indictments. When testifying before grand juries, some officers gave evasive answers, claiming ignorance about activities in the brothels. In contrast, police routinely testified about the brothels' character during the regulation system's monthly trials in the municipal court. Officials, then, manipulated the law so as to maintain the system of regulation and block reform efforts.

Morality and legality aside, officials explained their commitment to regulation in terms of the policy's practicality. It gave the police some control over the illicit marketplace, minimizing violence, theft, disease, and disorder. In contrast, an aggressive policy of prohibition threatened to drive prostitution underground, eliminating police supervision of vice. But did these practical concerns adequately account for the officials' determination to regulate?

Two arguments suggest that officials had an economic interest in regulation. The first possibility is that the officials were corrupt, bribed by madams to leave the brothels alone. In 1870, a police court witness testified that Mary E. Robinson "boasted that she was not afraid of the new city government. She could buy up the city officers now, the same as she had before."[6] (Robinson may have been referring to the years before regulation went into effect in 1863; she had been in St. Paul—presumably operating a brothel—since 1854.) Fifteen years later, the *Pioneer Press*'s pre-election attack on Rice's mayoral campaign warned: "A regime under which gambling and like illicit ventures flourish is harvest time for policemen who are officers for what they can make out of it. They divide the swag with the law-breaker, and draw a handsome revenue from the contributions of protected crime."[7]

These comments are the most direct claims that vice enforcement in St. Paul was corrupt; specific abuses did not come to public attention. Perhaps bribery was widespread but went unreported through the ignorance, discretion, or complicity of the press. But it seems more likely that regulation inhibited, rather than invited, corruption in St. Paul. Officials made no secret of their policy. There was, then, no public expectation that the police would drive the brothels out of business, and this in turn must have reduced the officers' power to do madams favors and ignore their operations in return for bribes. Fifty years after O'Brien's administration, a reporter wrote a history of St. Paul's political machine, arguing that, in 1880, vice enforcement was not corrupt: "There was practically no graft in the city hall. . . . But graft in the sense of the outright paying of money for . . . special privilege was unknown. . . . gambling, which was rampant, was not subject to graft. True, only the favored few were allowed to run gambling houses, but, every game was run on the square."[8] Certainly there is no evidence that corruption under regulation was more widespread than that found when social control agents were publicly committed to prohibiting vice.

The second claim of economic interest involves the fines paid by madams. Reformers sometimes charged that officials regulated vice as a source of revenue. While money did flow into the city treasury, the madams' fines represented only a tiny fraction of St. Paul's civic revenue. Moreover, the officials who repeatedly defended regulation on several grounds never mentioned its value as a revenue source. Overall, the evidence supports the conclusion that officials regulated vice largely because they found it an effective means of social control, and not because they had an economic interest in the system.

Still, one embarrassing question remains: Why did the police regularly arrest and fine prostitutes but allow gamblers free rein? The press remarked about the different treatment gamblers received, as did citizens in their letters to the editor and reformers in their crusades. When Mayor O'Brien took office, St. Paul's seven plush gambling "hells" employed between fifty and one hundred people—a vice industry nearly the size of the demimonde. O'Brien's order that the police close both the gambling hells and the brothels was the first serious attempt to halt gambling in the city.

Earlier antigambling enforcement efforts consisted of sporadic raids, usually after the press or an angry citizen demanded that the police do something. In addition, officials occasionally interceded when customers complained of heavy losses, forcing the gamblers to return the money. In their limited efforts to minimize cheating, the police arrested one gambler found using cogged (or loaded) dice, and they actively pursued the teams of criminals who played three-card monte, the centuries-old confidence trick disguised as a card game. But, for the most part, gamblers operated without interference.[9]

The officials' failure to either prohibit or systematically regulate gambling reflected a double standard of justice. The arrest ledger showed twenty-two men arrested for gambling; ten were professional gamblers, but there were also four merchants, three showmen, two saloon employees, a tailor, and a barber. Those charged with gambling tended to be well-established figures—married, native-born, over thirty, and, excluding the professional gamblers, in skilled trades or the middle class.[10] Perhaps the police chose to ignore gambling whenever possible because it involved relatively prominent men. Just as the officials did not bother the brothels' male customers or landlords, they left the men in the gambling hells alone.

Prohibition Triumphs

By 1885, when Edmund Rice replaced Christopher O'Brien as St. Paul's mayor and began regulating the brothels again, prostitution occupied a less visible place in the city. St. Paul continued to grow rapidly; its population reached 133,000 in 1890, 163,000 in 1900, and 215,000 in 1910. The police force grew along with the city; there were 178 officers in 1890, 267 in 1910.[11] Local news, confined to a column or two in the four-page dailies of the 1870s, now covered several pages, while stories about madams and prostitutes were now less common, so that news about vice occupied a much less prominent place in the city's newspapers.

St. Paul's population increase, coupled with its growing police resources, including not only more officers but improved communications and transportation, led to a dramatic increase in arrests that further diminished the relative importance of prostitution as a police problem. In the early 1870s, the department averaged 3.1 arrests per day (about 1,130 per year); prostitution accounted for over 10 percent of those arrests. In 1890, police made 5,277 arrests (including 228 for prostitution offenses, 4.3 percent of the total); by 1910, prostitution accounted for only 188 (3.3 percent) of the city's 5,781 arrests.[12]

St. Paul's police remained politicized throughout the period before World War I. Appointment to the force was a form of patronage. Between 1889 and 1913, St. Paul elected a mayor of a different political party than his predecessor on five occasions; four of those years saw the appointment of a new police chief (in the fifth case, a chief of long standing was allowed to keep his post, but he later resigned, complaining of political interference). On years when the mayor's party changed, an average of 48.2 new officers joined the force, compared to 19.9 newcomers in years when the same party retained the mayor's office. By 1900, Richard T. "The Cardinal" O'Connor controlled the city's Democratic machine; his brother, John J. O'Connor, was chief of police from 1900 to 1911. In alliance with local businessmen, they established the "O'Connor System"—"a scheme by which criminals across the country were told that they would not be arrested in St. Paul as long as they obeyed the law while within the city."[13] The system had its advocates; a 1912 History of the St. Paul Police Department argued that, under "the master hand of John J. O'Connor . . . St. Paul . . . has been the quietest town from a police standpoint of any place of even one half its size in America."[14]

As might be expected, prostitution continued to be regulated in St. Paul throughout this period, with occasional interruptions when reformers prodded officials into brief crackdowns: "The [license] system, interrupted now and again by reform movements and changes of administration, continued throughout the 1890s and, to some degree, after the turn of the century. In 1890 St. Paul health officials proposed a program of medical examination for prostitutes, but this was opposed by Presbyterian ministers."[15] In 1903, there was "a crusade against the keepers of disorderly houses," and "on June 10th, 1907, St. Paul enjoyed its first Sunday with an absolutely air-tight lid on," but these were brief, intermittent reforms, much like the earlier campaign of Judge Howard.[16] As St. Paul grew, vice enforcement became less public, less visible.

We know more about what happened in Minneapolis during this

same period: "Minneapolis went through a similar cycle of reforms, followed by a return to the license system."[17] St. Paul's twin city achieved national notoriety in 1903, when Lincoln Steffens published "The Shame of Minneapolis," one of his classic muckraking exposes in *McClure's Magazine*.[18] Steffens's target was the machine run by Mayor "Doc" Ames, and part of his analysis focused on how Ames had abused the city's system for regulating brothels by arrests. After appointing his brother chief of police, Ames ordered the city's madams arrested every other month rather than monthly as under the previous administration. However, during the months when the madams did not appear in court, Ames's agent visited the brothels and collected a bribe—equal to the usual fine. In addition, police extorted money from madams by making them purchase commemorative books, badges, and other favors.

Reformers drove Ames from office in 1902, and they announced a new vice policy: an end to regulating brothels through periodic arrests, their removal from residential and business districts, and "more strict control of bawdy-houses in the districts where they have been tolerated."[19] The next year brought further reforms; the new chief of police "gave upward of 35 women of the town . . . notice . . . they must either close out their places or remove the candy store fronts and remodel the buildings to correspond with other houses of this character in the proscribed district. It was a most radical reform. . . . The result today is that the street has been cleaned up, and now pedestrians, as they pass by, have no fear of being 'roped' or insulted by the inmates. Today there is little heard from the once notorious 'candy store' district."[20]

In 1910, reformers achieved a far greater triumph. City officials announced a broad commitment to prohibition: they ordered the red-light districts closed in April and, in November, "put into effect the drastic order prohibiting saloons from harboring prostitutes and directing the police to pursue a vigorous policy for the elimination of disorderly houses, wherever located in the city."[21] The following year, the Vice Commission of Minneapolis reported that the policy had been successful at minimizing prostitution in the city. Minneapolis would remain formally committed to a policy of prohibition.

The pattern evident in St. Paul and Minneapolis—decades of more-or-less public commitment to regulation, periodically challenged by reform campaigns that, over time, gained strength and ultimately triumphed—appeared in many cities during the Progressive

Era. Both locally and nationally, the late nineteenth century featured swelling opposition to prostitution. Earlier antiprostitution crusades, such as the antebellum Moral Reform Society or the Women's Christian Temperance Union–affiliated social purity movement, had had only limited successes, denouncing the double standard and blocking official plans to require medical inspections of prostitutes in St. Louis and elsewhere. However, in spite of the reformers' efforts, regulatory systems and segregated vice districts remained intact in St. Paul and most other cities into the beginning of the twentieth century.[22]

In most cities, effective campaigns for prohibition came only with the Progressive movement. Prostitution fit the Progressives' agenda: it was among the most visible of the urban problems that concerned them; it seemed to incorporate the twin evils of uncontrolled immigration and machine politics; it offered opportunities for the application of medical and social scientific expertise; and it could be addressed through a rhetoric of morality. As a consequence, the Progressives paid special attention to vice; their reform campaigns advanced simultaneously on several fronts. Physicians warned that the threat of venereal disease demanded an immediate solution but, unlike their nineteenth-century predecessors, many Progressive doctors now allied themselves with moral reformers, arguing that prohibition was the only answer. The Progressives established local vice commissions in Minneapolis and other cities that exposed the evils of red-light districts and called for an end to official toleration of the illicit marketplace.

Under the Progressive reformers' pressure, officials halted local systems of regulation, but, where the nineteenth century often had featured temporary pauses in regulation, these were permanent policy changes. Concern about white slavery reached new levels, leading to the Mann Act's passage. Mark Thomas Connelly argues that prostitution was important to the Progressives because it served as a symbol for a diffuse set of national concerns:

> The United States was transformed from a predominantly rural-minded, decentralized, principally Anglo-saxon, production-oriented, and morally absolutist society to a predominantly urban, centralized, multi-ethnic, consumption-oriented, secular, and relativist society . . . . This transformation is generally regarded as forward-looking

and modernizing. It was accompanied, however, by contrapuntal themes of tension, anxiety, and fear. The response to prostitution constituted just such a theme, for it expressed, and was propelled by, grave misgivings about the manifestations and consequences of that reorientation. . . . the most salient characteristics of the response to prostitution were confusion and bewilderment; it was an American expression of modernization and its discontents.[23]

The movement's climax came with America's involvement in World War I. Joining the war announced the emergence of the United States as a modern, international power. Consistent with Connelly's thesis, reformers' anxiety about vice reached its peak during the war. They warned that the decent, pure, young men who marched off to defend democracy were threatened by moral and physical contamination from prostitutes. Reformers now characterized the red-light districts near every major Army and Navy base, long justified as both serving the servicemen's needs and protecting local civilians, as threats to the country's youth, sources of pollution that jeopardized America's future. Public outcry demanded prohibition to protect the troops' health and morals; regulation or segregation was no longer acceptable. The authorities closed the major vice districts, one after the other. Federal pressure speeded the process where military installations were nearby; elsewhere, local reformers made themselves felt. By 1920, prohibition had triumphed; in virtually every city, official toleration of vice ended.[24]

The Impact of Prohibition

According to social historian John C. Burnham, "the most striking tangible alteration in American social life in the Progressive era was the decline of the traditional red light or segregated district in American cities."[25] However, the impact of this change needs to be assessed with some care. Regulation's defenders had warned that prohibition would not end vice; rather, vice would be driven underground, spreading prostitution throughout the city, increasing venereal disease, and leading to crimes of violence and theft. Were these predications borne out? Did prohibition policies prove to be the greater of two evils? These questions are surprisingly hard to answer because historians find it easier to study prostitution in 1875 or 1900 than in 1925. Under regulation, officials in cities such as St.

Paul produced records of arrests and newspapers gave prostitution considerable coverage; at the beginning of the new century, the Progressives' vice commissions conducted surveys of prostitutes and published volumes of information. Closing the red-light districts, however, not only hid prostitution from those citizens whom it offended, it also reduced what was written about vice, blocking the historian's view. As a consequence, any discussion of vice after World War I must be tentative, laced with qualifications.

In New York, prohibition pushed some prostitutes toward the control of organized crime. Thomas Dewey, while a special prosecutor, charged that a syndicate led by Charles "Lucky" Luciano centralized brothel prostitution in New York in 1933. The city's vice was already relatively centralized: independent bookers offered scheduling services (after a week or so in one brothel, a prostitute could call a booker, who would place her in a different house which had an opening), while independent bonders charged each prostitute $10 per week in return for a guarantee that they would make bond if the woman was arrested. Luciano's syndicate took over both operations, forcing the independent bookers and bonders to either join the syndicate or quit the business. Worse, the syndicate charged more and delivered less than its predecessors. This was systematic extortion, "based solely on terror." Faced with threats of violence, madams, inmates, bookers, and bonders surrendered to Luciano.[26] Such extortionate relationships can form the basis for organized crime's control over illicit marketplaces. A large, centralized organization may offer some advantages of scale, but, advantages aside, under some conditions the organization can exact compliance from madams, bookies, and other underground entrepreneurs merely by threatening them with violence or harassment by corrupt officials who will do the organization's bidding. The typical madam lacks the resources to defend her brothel from the threatened attacks, and, under prohibition, she cannot turn to the authorities for aid.[27]

Not every city displayed this pattern of increasingly centralized vice. Prostitution in San Francisco remained an industry of independent entrepreneurs; if anything, the city's brothels were more likely to be independent after prohibition took effect. During the nineteenth century, San Francisco's prostitution was concentrated in Chinatown, where tongs controlled many brothels. Prohibition "resulted in prostitutes scattering throughout the city, creating a 'red light non-district' or a 'non-zone of prostitution.'"[28] This dispersion coincided with the rise of tourism and the decline of tong-controlled vice as the economic foundation for Chinatown. Under prohibition, individual madams made their own arrangements with San Francisco authorities, paying bribes to be left alone.

In contrast, Chicago resembled New York; criminal syndicates took advantage of their corrupt ties with the police to bring the brothels in the old vice districts further under their control. But Chicago had a history of centralized vice working in coordination with the political machine. Moreover, not all prostitutes fell under the syndicates' control. In his classic analysis of the impact of reform, Reckless found that, as in San Francisco, new, smaller brothels spread outside Chicago's traditional vice districts, operating for short periods at an address before moving, and that independent prostitutes also increased.[29]

These examples—New York, San Francisco, Chicago—involve large cities with long-notorious vice districts; it is not unreasonable to suspect that these cities may have been atypical. There are relatively few studies of twentieth-century prostitution following the implementation of prohibition; however, the evidence from the major cities suggests that prohibition's critics were at least partially correct. Instead of eliminating vice, reform dispersed it into more neighborhoods, while increasing official corruption and, in some cities, the influence of organized crime. Yet these new problems did not cause as much public outrage as the Progressives had mustered against tolerating vice. Public awareness of prostitution as a major social problem fell throughout most of the twentieth century; prohibition did not have as many vocal critics as the policies it replaced. Moreover, this decline in public concern seems to have paralleled a real decline in at least some forms of prostitution; the brothel, in particular, became less common. Was prohibition, then, a success?[30]

Prohibition's apparent success was probably due less to its own advantages than to social changes that reduced the demand for prostitution in general and for brothels in particular. First, demographic changes made women less scarce. In 1910, the United States contained 106.2 males for every 100 females. This ratio dropped in each successive decade; by 1950, women were a majority. Second, sexual customs changed: premarital sex became more common; and the rate of intercourse within marriage rose. Third, more men married. The nineteenth-century "bachelor subculture" gave gambling hells, saloons, pool halls, and brothels a ready supply of customers; as more men traded bachelor independence for married domesticity, the demand for vice dropped. Prostitution, of course, never disappeared; it only changed form. Reduced demand, coupled with social control campaigns, pushed criminal syndicates out of brothel prostitution and into more profitable rackets. Streetwalking continued, although the nature of the offense makes it especially difficult to measure changes in its incidence. Call girls—and later massage parlors—emerged as the modern counterparts to brothel prostitution. To these changes, add the development of effective cures for venereal diseases, and it becomes clear why prohibition never had long-term consequences as disastrous as the regulationists predicted for it.[31]

By the 1960s, prostitution had nearly dropped from public notice. Most call girls operated with minimal interference from the police. What time the police did devote to vice was spent controlling streetwalkers. Modern citizens, like their nineteenth-century counterparts, found visible prostitution offensive; they objected to streetwalkers in front of their businesses or near their homes. In response, most police departments concentrated on keeping streetwalking within what were unofficial but generally accepted boundaries, occasionally cracking down completely when public complaints drew attention. Depending on departmental practices and priorities, vice squad officers might exploit their position by collecting bribes for leaving prostitutes alone or dedicated officers might enter into the frustrating game of trying to make legal vice arrests. These variations fell within a general pattern: the past, with its segregated districts and regulatory systems, was forgotten; police and public took prohibition for granted. They understood its limitations, and they accepted them.[32]

This complacency, like so much else, was challenged by the feminist movement. In *The Politics of Deviance*, Edwin M. Schur suggests that the women's movement became an umbrella constituency under which a broad-based group (women) could articulate concerns about many social issues, each directly affecting only a minority of its members. Thus, prostitution, as well as other forms of deviance involving women, such as lesbianism, rape, and abortion, became defined as issues of concern to feminists, who hoped to effect changes by bringing the influence of large numbers of women to bear on each of these issues.[33]

Feminist sociological analyses of prostitution evolved in several directions, sometimes creating contradictory positions. Yet they share the underlying idea that modern prostitution is organized so as to leave women at a disadvantage; as Barbara Heyl suggests: "It may well be that the oldest profession is the most sexist of them all."[34] For instance, Kathleen Barry emphasizes involuntary prostitution as an important form of female sexual slavery; she focuses on the prostitute as an unwilling victim of exploitative pimps and violent customers. Other feminist analysts, however, argue that women voluntarily choose prostitution and other sex work as the most attractive jobs available in an economy that blocks them from most desirable employment opportunities. The double standard of justice, which ignores customers and the landlords who profit from vice but punishes prostitutes, comes under attack, as do police corruption, police harassment and entrapment, and the constitutionality of vice laws. Such critiques identify flaws in prohibition's operation.

Feminists' efforts to affect vice policy currently focus on raising the public's consciousness of prostitution as an issue. The most visible force in this campaign has been COYOTE, sometimes described as "the hookers' union." Ultimately, most feminists advocate decriminalization: criminal laws against prostitution would be eliminated, but vice would be regulated through laws governing zoning, licensing, health inspections, and so on. These policy proposals advocate minimal interference with the marketplace for vice, beyond geographic restrictions, limits on underage prostitutes, and other basic ground rules. These new regulators' calls for an end to prohibition have not, as yet, created widespread public concern about vice policy. What the future holds, of course, remains unclear. But currently, inertia and apathy seem to be powerful allies of prohibition.[35]

Summary

During the second half of the nineteenth century, most urban officials tried to be realistic about prostitution policy. They believed that they were incapable of successfully prohibiting vice and that, in fact, vigorous prohibitionist efforts were likely to make things worse. In St. Paul, and in dozens of other cities, the authorities adopted segregation and other forms of regulation as a practical solution to this dilemma. If vice could not be prohibited, it could at least be constrained. Reformers attacked the officials' stance, arguing that regulatory policies were morally bankrupt, but the officials held off the reform campaigns. At the turn of the century, red-light districts and other forms of regulated vice remained a standard feature on the urban landscape.

The twentieth-century history of American prostitution begins with the Progressives' reform campaigns against existing policies of regulation. The campaigns' success left social control agents officially committed to prohibition, although their enthusiasm for the new policy often was limited. Prohibition's initial impact was modest; brothels moved but stayed open, although organized crime sometimes had more influence over their operation. However, as the demand for prostitution fell, the dominant form of prostitution shifted toward call girls and streetwalkers. The police concentrated on the latter, and prostitution became an issue of little concern to most people. As this century ends, however, there are new clamors for reform—this time from feminists concerned with prostitution's exploitation of women. These new reformers advocate a return to policies of regulation. The oscillating demands for reform—first through prohibition, then through regulation—reaffirm the difficulties of controlling illicit marketplaces.

The history of American efforts to control prostitution over the last century and a half reveals the need for more rigorous analysis of social control strategies. By focusing on control agents' day-to-day tactics, sociologists have ignored the workings and consequences of broader social control strategies. It is necessary to compare different strategies in action. Further, a more systematic analytic framework is needed to understand the process by which social control strategies are established and changed. In particular, analysts should reconsider the roles of morality and practicality in policy making. These issues are examined in the final chapter.

7

SOCIAL CONTROL: STRATEGY, PRACTICALITY, AND MORALITY

Most sociological studies of deviance examine forms of rule-break-ing—crime, substance abuse, sexual misbehavior, and the like—that fall under the purview of the police. This shapes the analysts' thinking, leading many sociologists of deviance to view police as typical social control agents and, because police rhetoric empha-sizes the prohibition of crime, to make an implicit assumption that social control policies normally aim to eradicate deviance. Thus, Gary T. Marx writes of "ironies of social control," "where social control contributes to, or even generates, rule-breaking behavior."[1] To consider such situations ironic, of course, we must assume that eradication is the normal, overt goal of social control. But not all control efforts seek to eliminate or prohibit deviance; the local sys-tems for regulating prostitution in St. Paul and other nineteenth-century cities are obvious exceptions. Such arrangements do not fit neatly into our standard frameworks for analyzing deviance and so-cial control; we suspect that these systems must have been corrupt or, at best, hypocritical—suspicions that ignore the forthright, cal-culated nature of many of these policies.

In short, the sociology of deviance has not paid sufficient atten-tion to alternative strategies for social control. Agents' narrower tactical choices have received considerable attention, but analysts often take broad strategic approaches to policy for granted, simply assuming that social control agents try to eliminate deviance through a strategy of prohibition. Yet alternative strategies exist. Two—prevention and regulation—are important enough to warrant systematic comparison to prohibition.[2]

Three Social Control Strategies

The discussion that follows treats prohibition, prevention, and regulation as ideal types, offering broad generalizations about each strategy's overall goals, its principal tactics, the standard methods for evaluating its relative success or failure, and its vulnerability to criticism. The policymakers that set social control policies and the social control agents who carry out those policies rarely think in these abstract terms. In design and especially in practice, social control policies often incorporate elements from different strategies. However, before addressing those complexities, it will help to consider each strategy as an ideal type.

Prohibition

Prohibition is a social control strategy that aims to eliminate and forbid deviance by sanctioning (usually punishing) offenders. After an offense occurs, social control agents must complete several intermediate steps—learning about the offense and identifying, locating, and apprehending the offender—before they can levy sanctions. For example, when a rape victim complains to the police, officers investigate to learn the rapist's identity and location, leading to his arrest, trial, conviction, and sentencing. In theory, effective social control will minimize, if not eradicate, rape by deterring prospective rapists.

Eradication need not be complete for prohibition to be considered successful; the policy serves several other purposes. Sanctioning deviants provides retribution; it returns the moral order to a balance by making the offender suffer costs that presumably equal or outweigh whatever benefits he or she gained from deviance. Prohibition also can be corrective; being sanctioned may teach the offender not to repeat the deviant act—the effect sometimes called specific deterrence. Such correction may depend on the deviant acquiring new motives: punitive sanctions may cause the offender to fear the consequences of committing further offenses, while thera-peutic sanctions may lead the treated or reeducated deviant to rede-fine the deviant act as inappropriate or undesirable. In addition to discouraging the deviant from recidivism, public sanctioning may deter other potential offenders—what is called general deterrence. Thus, the spectacle of an offender being sanctioned teaches others the risks of deviance; once they recognize the likelihood of being sanctioned, potential deviant acts may not seem worthwhile.[3]

Prohibition is the standard control policy in our culture. Its as-sumptions guide most control agents' thinking most of the time. In part, this is because prohibition is more common and more visible than alternative social control strategies. The contemporary Ameri-can criminal justice and mental health systems, whatever their dif-ferences, share prohibition as their primary control strategy. After all, prohibition is a supremely practical response to deviance. De-viant acts—violations of major social norms—cannot be ignored; they demand some reaction to demonstrate society's reaffirmation of those norms. Prohibition fills this need.

Prohibition is a broad strategy that encompasses various tactics. One major tactical distinction is whether control agents concen-trate on identifying offenders or offenses.[4] When the authorities usually receive reports of offenses, agents can work at learning the offenders' identities, responding to complaints about deviance with investigations and sanctioning. This is reactive social control: the agents' actions depend upon receiving and reacting to a prior com-plaint. In contrast, some offenses rarely get reported; if agents are to sanction these deviants, they must first discover the offenses. When agents search for evidence that deviance is occurring, as in police undercover operations, they engage in proactive social control. The need for proactive measures varies with the type of offense. Nor-mally, victims complain when they are exploited; where there is no immediate victim, as in the various forms of vice, complaints are rare and proactive efforts more common. Proactive social control carries risks. The investigations must be kept secret from the de-viants, and this secrecy also conceals the agents' actions from their supervisors and the public. Because they cannot be observed, agents may commit illicit acts of their own, abusing their powers or taking bribes. These problems are not confined to proactive social control, but they are less often associated with reactive measures.

Social control agencies that pursue policies of prohibition find it relatively easy to evaluate the effectiveness of their operations. Two standard measures exist. First, agents can count the number of deviant acts that come to their attention, thereby measuring the incidence of deviance. The best known measure of incidence is the crime rate, based on the number of crimes known to the police. Because incidence statistics are indirect measures of effectiveness, they can be interpreted to the agents' advantage. Agents who can point to a decline in the incidence of deviance can take credit for being effective (ignoring the possibility that the decline had some other cause). On the other hand, an increase in the incidence of deviance can be seen as occurring in spite of the agents' best efforts; they can argue that they should not be held to blame for the increase and, further, that they need greater resources to combat the growing threat of deviance.

A second measure of prohibition's effectiveness is the proportion of deviant acts that lead to sanctioning. In police work, this is the clearance rate—the proportion of known crimes leading to an arrest. Measures of both incidence and sanctioning are subject to important inaccuracies; both depend on how often agents learn about deviance, and this, in turn, depends on the agents' resources and their methods of gathering and interpreting information.[5] Offenses that do not come to the agents' attention—or that for some other reason are not included in the officials' tally—lead to inaccurate measures of effectiveness. These inaccuracies become particularly severe when agents must depend on proactive tactics because relatively few offenses come to their attention. Although evaluating policies of prohibition involves difficulties of interpretation and accuracy, these problems pale when compared to the difficulty of evaluating the effectiveness of other social control strategies.

Prevention

If prohibition is the standard, taken-for-granted social control strategy, prevention seems to be the most attractive alternative. Prevention aims to keep deviance from occurring. In theory, a successful preventive program offers important benefits: it reduces the incidence of deviance, minimizing the threat to the society, thereby reducing the need for social control agents engaged in prohibition. While these are important benefits, preventive policies have serious practical limitations that keep them from being widely adopted as agents' primary social control strategies.

Like prohibition, prevention can involve a range of tactics. At the most concrete level, preventive tactics block opportunities for deviance; at a more abstract level, the tactics seek to block the motivation to commit deviant acts. Blocking opportunities—sometimes called target-hardening—makes it more difficult to commit deviant acts.[6] Target-hardening increases the offenders' risks or reduces their chances for success. The homeowner who installs a deadbolt lock, the city transit system that forbids bus drivers from carrying cash, and the police who patrol neighborhoods at night are all engaged in target-hardening. Some of these programs are inexpensive; prohibiting bus drivers from carrying cash prevents them from being robbed at no cost except inconvenience to passengers who must remember to carry the correct change. On the other hand, target-hardening can be costly; to protect the president from attack, the U.S. Secret Service has an elaborate—and very expensive—preventive program.

Even more expensive are preventive tactics aimed at blocking motivation to commit deviant acts. While blocking opportunities tries to deter deviance, blocking motivation tries to induce respectable behavior. Here, social control agents develop a theory of deviance causation and then design tactics to interfere with this causal process. For example, in response to the theory that deviants are frustrated by limited opportunities for respectable work, agents may offer job training as a deviance prevention program. Or agents who believe that deviants lack moral values may advocate religious training as a preventive measure. The agents assume that these tactics can keep individuals—who might otherwise choose to commit deviant acts—within the bounds of respectability. However, because agents usually cannot specify which individuals are in jeopardy of becoming deviant, these social control programs tend to define many people as potential offenders, thereby raising the cost of prevention.[7]

It is very difficult to evaluate the effectiveness of preventive social control programs. Presumably, a totally effective program is one under which deviant acts do not occur; more realistically, most programs hope to reduce the incidence of deviance. But it is hard to measure what does not happen. While agents often are quick to attribute declines in the incidence of deviance to their preventive activities, another cause may be at work. Agents' claims of effectiveness can be tested only by using sophisticated experimental designs to measure the programs' impact.[8] Occasionally, agents conduct these experiments, but most simply take credit for any decline in deviance. Or, if the incidence of deviance does not decline, agents may still argue that preventive programs are successful, claiming that the incidence would be even greater but for the programs' effects. To support these claims, agents may offer anecdotal evidence for the program's impact or supply organizational measures that document the program's scope, for instance, by counting the hours worked by agents. Such organizational measures have the virtue of being quantifiable, but they reflect tautological reasoning. They do not measure effectiveness unless one first assumes that the program is effective and that organizational measures are an index of its impact. In most cases, neither incidence nor organizational measures can prove conclusively that preventive programs are effective.

The difficulty in measuring the effectiveness of preventive social control makes these programs especially vulnerable to attack. When they are inexpensive, criticism is muted. But costly programs, particularly those aimed at blocking motivations for deviance, need to prove their worth. A job training program may keep some trainees from committing crimes, but that effect is hard to demonstrate. Probably some trainees would not have committed crimes in any case, and others may commit crimes in spite of the program. Such programs return an unknown and arguably slight benefit. The agents' inability to prove their programs' effect on incidence leads them to rely on organizational measures for justification, yet determined critics cannot be convinced by these indirect measures. As a consequence, deviance prevention is a popular goal, but it rarely becomes the primary basis for social control policy, unless the tactics chosen are inexpensive.

Regulation

The third major social control strategy is regulation. Regulation seeks to control some of the circumstances of the deviant act. Regulation often arises out of the failures of prohibition and prevention. It involves an overt compromise: recognizing that they cannot prohibit or prevent some form of deviance, social control agents agree to permit the disapproved act to occur, so long as they can control some of its features. For example, the American experience with Prohibition convinced most officials that drinking could not be eradicated. Repeal decriminalized alcohol use, but most states immediately passed laws regulating the minimum drinking age, the licensing of vendors, and so on. While legal, drinking retains a tainted moral status; the policy of regulation restricts the circumstances under which it can occur.[9]

The example of regulating alcohol typifies the natural history of this social control strategy. Regulation becomes an attractive solution when a widespread offense cannot be prohibited or prevented. Typically, for reasons discussed below, this involves an illicit marketplace in which a forbidden good or service is exchanged. Examples include prostitution, gambling, pornography, illicit drugs, and other deviant exchanges between willing participants.[10] If agents can neither reduce the demand for the good or service nor halt the supply, continued deviance is inevitable. Prohibition's failure became obvious when the authorities could not stop alcohol manufacture and distribution and citizens continued to buy and drink alcohol. If deviance is inevitable, regulation, which at least promises some control over the marketplace, may come to be seen as desirable.

However, the turn toward regulation may also reflect the constellation of vested interests in deviance. In his book *Bad Habits*, the social historian John C. Burnham argues that Prohibition's ineffectiveness did not, in itself, lead to the policy's repeal. Rather, the alcohol industry mounted a calculated campaign for Repeal and the regulation of alcohol. In Burnham's view, claims that Prohibition failed ignored the policy's real success in reducing overall levels of alcohol consumption. Instead, industry proponents found allies among officials who saw legal, regulated alcohol as a prospective source of tax revenue, and they mounted a slick public relations campaign emphasizing Prohibition's shortcomings and touting Repeal and regulation.[11] Without assessing the relative role of vested interests in constructing Prohibition as a failure, it is clear that collective memory now treats the policy as a failed experiment, and advocates of regulation often draw parallels with alcohol policy.

Regulatory tactics vary with the offense. Common tactics include excluding some customers from the illicit marketplace (as in laws barring minors from buying cigarettes), limiting the number and character of suppliers (as in liquor licensing), and supervising the quality of the good or service (as in medical inspection of prostitutes). The choice of tactics depends upon how the offense is thought to threaten the society; agents may try to block the corruption of innocents, the involvement of criminals in the marketplace, and so on.

While there is wide variation in regulatory tactics, two general thrusts can be identified. First, some regulatory programs concentrate on protecting customers from exploitation. Customers may become morally tainted by entering the illicit marketplace, but they retain their rights to social control agents' protection; agents try to keep them from being cheated, attacked, or otherwise victimized. Here, agents work to keep potentially exploitative suppliers out of the marketplace; they also may supervise the quality of the good or service, limit the customers' liability to the suppliers, and respond to customers' complaints of unfair treatment. English gambling laws, which strictly limit the ways players can be recruited and the circumstances of play, are an example of regulation protecting customers.[12]

Second, agents can regulate the marketplace, keeping it orderly and thereby protecting the suppliers' interests. These tactics include limiting the number of suppliers, making sure that no supplier has an unfair competitive advantage, and protecting suppliers against exploitation by customers. The agents who regulate gambling in Nevada cooperate with the casinos to protect the gaming industry that accounts for much of that state's revenue.[13] Of course, the distinction between regulation to protect customers and regulation to protect suppliers is largely analytical; regulatory policies usually involve both elements, although agents may place greater emphasis on one or the other.

It is difficult to measure the effectiveness of regulation. The strategy is designed to minimize problems associated with a morally tainted activity. These effects are hard to measure; to what degree does legalized gambling reduce cheating and other problems associated with unregulated games? (And, its critics ask, what are the costs of legalization—the lives ruined by greater access to gambling and so on?) In the face of such evaluation problems, agents again tend to offer organizational measures to demonstrate their worth.

Organizational measures also suit a subtle change in focus that affects many regulatory programs. Because the regulated marketplace is morally tainted, some respectable citizens object to regulation, which they see as a policy that supports or at least tolerates deviance. Because illicit marketplaces typically charge high prices, regulation usually reduces costs to customers. It is therefore possible to convert regulation to a source of revenue by taxing suppliers or customers.[14] Taxation makes regulation self-supporting, or even profitable, giving officials a vested interest in the policy and minimizing complaints from respectable citizens. So long as the tax's cost does not raise prices above those in the unregulated, underground marketplace, customers also benefit. However, taxing the regulated market for revenue creates an opportunity for a new form of deviance—cheating the tax collector—and agents charged with regulation must vigilantly patrol the marketplace to ensure full payment. At this point, regulation can fade in importance as agents work to prohibit or prevent cheating on taxes. Organizational measures, such as the number of licensed suppliers or total tax revenue, become important, not so much because they measure the effectiveness of controlling deviance through regulation but because they reflect the tax collectors' diligence.

Prohibition, prevention, and regulation are alternative strategies for coping with deviance. They differ in the means by which they achieve control, as well as their rationales, tactics, methods for evaluating effectiveness, and public acceptability (see table 7.1). To a large extent, they coexist and even overlap; social control agents often adopt different strategies to deal with different offenses. American police pursue a policy of prohibition in responding to predatory

Table 7.1
Three Social Control Strategies

	Strategy		
	Prohibition	*Prevention*	*Regulation*
Means of control	bring sanctions against deviant acts	keep deviant acts from occurring	control circumstances of deviant acts
Principal tactics	a. reactive b. proactive	a. block opportunities b. block motivation	a. protect customers b. protect suppliers
Principal methods of evaluation	a. incidence rate b. sanctioning rate	a. incidence rate b. organizational measures	a. organizational measures b. tax compliance
Vulnerability to criticism	low	high (expense)	high (morality)

crimes, but their routine patrols—and whatever general deterrent effect their arrests have—promote crime prevention. Further, some of the laws they enforce, such as those governing drinking, are part of a regulatory policy. The police, the legislators who write the criminal codes, and the public understand that social control policies must be tailored to fit different offenses.

However, this general consensus about social control strategy often disappears in debates over how to deal with a particular offense. Since the 1960s, policy debates have surrounded attempts to control marijuana, cocaine, and other drugs, as well as prostitution, premarital sexuality, homosexuality, abortion, pornography, and gambling. Social movements of deviants, such as the National Organization for the Reform of Marijuana Laws (marijuana smokers) and COYOTE (prostitutes), demand regulation or decriminalization. Opposing movements, such as Right to Life (opposed to abortion) and Citizens for Decent Literature (opposed to pornography), advocate policies of prohibition. These contentious offenses share an underlying organization; they involve deviant exchanges, occurring in illicit marketplaces. These policy debates arise because deviant exchanges are particularly difficult to control.

Deviant Exchange and Regulation

Regardless of which social control strategy agents choose, deviant exchanges pose difficulties. Efforts to prohibit deviant exchanges are particularly prone to failure; it is almost a sociological truism that illicit marketplaces cannot be eradicated. The need to discover deviant transactions forces agents to adopt proactive tactics, such as undercover investigations to infiltrate the illicit marketplace, and proactive tactics have important limitations. First, their impact varies with the agents' resources; unless many agents are assigned to the task, they are unlikely to discover the illicit marketplace's full extent; while agents may disrupt portions of the illicit network, those segments that the investigators do not expose will continue to operate. Second, discreet deviants can protect their exchanges; by conducting their exchanges in private places, limiting their dealings to partners they know and trust, and keeping their illicit activities secret, determined deviants can prevent social control agents from penetrating their segment of the illicit marketplace. The more discreet the deviants, the less effective the agents' efforts. Third, when deviant sales generate substantial profits, agents may be corrupted. Because proactive tactics are hard to supervise, agents can safely ignore some deviant exchanges in return for cash bribes, free goods or services from sellers, or information. The familiar news stories of narcotics officers taking bribes, dealing confiscated drugs, or protecting criminal informants illustrate this problem. Confronted with the need for proactive tactics, limited resources, discretion by offenders, and the temptations of corruption, attempts to prohibit deviant exchanges seem doomed.[15]

Like prohibition, preventive campaigns usually cannot halt deviant exchange. Sometimes agents try to block opportunities for deviant exchanges by disrupting the supply of the forbidden good or service. For example, antidrug campaigns may ignore the drug buyer in favor of attacking the dealers' distribution network. This preventive policy (blocking buyers' opportunities to obtain drugs) depends upon eradicating the drug traffic. Here, as elsewhere, agents distinguish between customers and sellers in deviant exchanges. Sellers are viewed as committing more serious offenses because they act deliberately and make a monetary profit. In contrast, customers may be portrayed as relative innocents, corrupted by temptation. Attempts to disrupt supply exaggerate the disadvantages of proactive attempts to prohibit illicit marketplaces because sellers command more resources than their customers, making them better able to maintain discretion or corrupt social control agents. Unless pricing, distribution problems, or other features of the illicit traffic make it particularly vulnerable, social control agents usually cannot stop supplies from reaching the marketplace.[16]

Other preventive programs try to block motivations for deviance. Since people enter deviant exchanges voluntarily, they might be reeducated, taught to avoid the illicit marketplace. The nineteenth-century Temperance movement adopted this tactic; reformers sought to persuade drinkers to take the pledge against liquor. This program had its successes—many drinkers signed up—but the reformers could not convince everyone and, in frustration, they eventually turned to prohibition as a strategy. For any illicit marketplace, there will be prospective participants who can be convinced to stay away, as well as disenchanted people who are ready to leave. But people enter deviant exchanges because they expect to find them rewarding and, unless the preventive campaign can offer everyone acceptable substitute satisfactions, some deviants will continue to join in deviant exchanges.[17]

Regulation often emerges as a social control strategy precisely because prohibition and prevention cannot halt deviant exchanges. Its proponents argue that regulation promises several advantages. Often, they begin by charging that prohibition is an unprincipled goal when responding to deviant exchange. This libertarian argument emphasizes that participation in deviant exchange is voluntary and challenges social control agents' right to sanction individuals who decide to enter these transactions. The issue is central to political and social theory: when should the state (social control agents) interfere with the free choices of society's members? Regulators acknowledge that prohibition is appropriate for deviant exploitation, when deviants attack unwilling targets. But deviant exchanges feature only willing participants; there are no unwilling victims, so agents should not intervene.

Second, regulation's advocates note the failures of prohibition and prevention. These policies usually cannot eliminate deviant exchanges; even increasing social control resources cannot make these policies successful. When there is a demand for an illicit good or service, and someone is willing to supply that commodity, deviant exchange seems inevitable. Social control agents may drive the illicit marketplace underground, but they cannot eradicate it. Moreover, forcing deviant exchanges underground exacerbates the problem; removing the illicit marketplace from supervision leaves its participants free to exploit one another. Thus, the illicit market in heroin leads to several secondary problems: outrageously high prices for the drug; crimes committed by addicts to support their habits; high profits that attract organized criminals to the drug trade; drugs adulterated with dangerous substances; unsanitary practices that spread disease; police corruption and abuse of powers; and so on. Policies of prohibition tend to aggravate matters, increasing the social costs of the illicit marketplace.[18]

Furthermore, regulators sometimes charge that the social costs of deviant exchange are exaggerated, that the threat posed by the illicit marketplace is not as great as social control agents claim. For instance, laws against marijuana were originally justified by arguments that marijuana smokers were prone to violence and psychosis—claims now viewed as dubious. Regulation's advocates argue that, if the social costs of marijuana use are lower than once imagined, and if the costs of enforcing marijuana laws—agents' budgets, spreading contempt for the law, and so on—are higher, then the policy's value must be reassessed. Taken together, these points challenge the effectiveness of prohibition and prevention.

Finally, its advocates believe regulation has its own advantages. It offers social control agents better supervision over the illicit marketplace than existing policies; secondary problems can be reduced or eliminated when social control agents supervise deviant exchanges. And, if the exchanges are taxed, regulation can pay for itself; while prohibition drains social control agents' resources, regulation can become a source of revenue. In short, regulation is desirable because it does not interfere with individual freedom and because it promises better control and fewer secondary problems than rival social control strategies.[19]

These arguments do not go unchallenged. Regulation's opponents attack the policy on both principled and practical grounds. They question the policy's morality, emphasizing the values that underpin the rules against deviant exchange; norms against homosexuality, drug sales, and similar offenses reflect moral principles, and society should stand by those principles. Regulation is a compromise with immorality; it tolerates the intolerable. Prohibitionists acknowledge that policies of prohibition interfere with individuals' freedom of choice—and they applaud that interference: individuals should be kept from making immoral choices. On the practical side, prohibition's limitations do not justify abandoning the policy. Most social policies fall short of their objectives, but it is important for society to visibly strive toward those objectives and not be discouraged by failure. Further, prohibitionists argue that regulation is itself flawed. They charge that regulating deviant exchange will make the illicit marketplace more accessible and that some individuals who have been successfully deterred from entering deviant exchanges will, under regulation, become deviants. Regulating an illicit marketplace will spread deviance and associated forms of disorder through the society. Thus, legalizing abortion not only increases the number of abortions, it encourages sexual promiscuity and spreads venereal disease. For regulation's opponents, compromising on moral principles damages morale and weakens the larger social fabric.

The debate over regulation, then, has two themes—one practical, and the other principled. The practical debate centers on an empirical question: what are the consequences of different social control policies? Regulators argue that prohibition and prevention are inherently incapable of eliminating deviant exchange, while prohibitionists believe that increasing social control resources and raising the agents' priorities for the offenses in question could make prohibition and prevention successful. Similarly, regulation's opponents charge that that policy can only increase deviance, aggravating the problem. In rebuttal, proponents of regulation note that their policy is flexible, that regulatory rules can be tailored to constrain deviance by setting various limits on the marketplace and its participants.

The debate over principles involves competing values; it is a debate between those who place a higher value on individual freedom and those who place greater value on moral principles. Both values are part of the larger culture; they ordinarily coexist, but they are not necessarily consistent. For example, there is no clear compromise between the claim that a woman should control her own body and the counterclaim that abortion is murder. When debates are reduced to such ultimate moral judgments, participants rarely persuade one another. And, because they cannot be resolved, disputes over morality make regulatory policies perpetually vulnerable to their critics.

Morality, Practicality, and Policy

Contemporary sociologists sometimes downplay the role of morality in shaping social control, focusing instead on social control policy's service to important interests within society. Morality figured more prominently in classical sociological explanations that viewed social control as a response to deviants' violations of widely shared moral standards. However, following the emergence of labeling theory in the 1960s and critical criminology in the 1970s, most analysts have concentrated on exposing the interests that lie behind social control policy. In this view, social control becomes a tool for furthering society's dominant economic, political, and status interests. Thus, critical criminologist Richard Quinney argues, "Contrary to conventional wisdom, law instead of representing community customs is an instrument of the state that serves the interests of the developing capitalist ruling class."[20] The links to interests may be subtle; what seem to be debates over purely moral issues may conceal struggles among status interests. For instance, Joseph Gusfield views the nineteenth-century Temperance movement as a vehicle for preserving the dominance of the rural, Protestant, native-born middle class, and analogous interpretations can be made for contemporary moral debates over abortion, pornography, and marijuana.

This focus on interests threatens to ignore the real importance of morality in defining what is deviant and in symbolically justifying the use of sanctions. Morality is central to the rhetoric of control. Social control agents depend on an ideology of moral attitudes that explains and justifies the designation of some acts as respectable and others as deviant. Deviance is subject to sanctioning because ideology presents it as morally reprehensible; the use of sanctions is therefore justified. Further, applying sanctions through a "degradation ceremony" serves not only to label the offender as deviant but to reaffirm the existence of the moral standard and the society's commitment to that standard. Morality offers a rationale without which agents cannot act and the community cannot tolerate the agents' actions.[21]

Ideally, the rest of society's members share its agents' moral standards. This need not be the case; for instance, totalitarian governments can force their standards on people who do not believe in them. But democratic states depend upon a level of moral consensus; in theory, a large segment of the population should share the agents' standards, agreeing about what is respectable and what is not. Of course, the level of consensus varies from one form of deviance to another. Exploitative crimes of violence and theft are widely seen as serious offenses, meriting sanctions. At the other extreme are "folk crimes," prohibited by the authorities but tolerated by a substantial proportion of the population. Where moral consensus is absent, agents face challenges to the legitimacy of their policies.[22]

Illicit markets often become the focus for these challenges. As noted above, debates over deviant exchange address both principled and practical issues. Because both sellers and customers enter the marketplace voluntarily, critics can raise moral questions about the agents' right to interfere with these transactions. And, because illicit markets are especially difficult to control, the practicality of the agents' policy is also subject to attack. These challenges are not restricted to a particular social control strategy; both prohibition and regulation are vulnerable to criticism based on both principle and practicality.

On the one hand, when agents try to prohibit deviant exchange, people frustrated by the policy's failure—a group that often includes both buyers and sellers in the illicit marketplaces—apply pressure for regulation or even vindication. They want social control agents to stop—or at least reduce—their interference with the forbidden exchanges. COYOTE, the so-called "hookers' union" that advocates decriminalizing and licensing prostitution, is an example of a social movement advocating regulation. Typically, regulation advocates' rationales emphasize practicality, giving less weight to moral principles. Regulation's practical benefits reduce the problems associated with illicit marketplaces: when suppliers operate above ground prices drop; the quality of goods and services rises; corruption is minimized; and so on. In addition, regulation's advocates may debunk the supposed practical benefits of prohibition. For instance, laws against pornography were long justified by claims that pornography caused sex offenses. After 1970, however, the laws' critics argued for minimal regulation (i.e., restricting only minors' access to pornography), on the grounds that researchers sponsored by the U.S. Commission on Obscenity and Pornography could find no causal link between pornography and sex crimes.[23]

While regulators typically prefer to focus on issues of practicality, they cannot ignore questions of morality. Eradication's advocates point to the moral standards that underlie policies of prohibition; regulators must challenge those principles. They may do so by arguing that social control agents who pursue prohibition are misguided or overzealous absolutists—Puritans or bluenoses who interfere with what they should leave alone. Thus, Prohibition becomes an example of the misuse of official power: the state should not interfere with an adult's decision to drink, so long as drinking is done responsibly. Or advocates of regulation may justify their views with a higher principle; in the contemporary abortion debate, the pro-choice position holds that a woman's right to control her own body overrides the fetus's right to legal protection.

The strength of these moral arguments is reflected in the reformers' recommendations. When a strong, principled argument can be made against prohibition, reformers may advocate vindication (striking down all rules against some form of deviance), or they may recommend minimal regulation. Thus, an argument grounded in First Amendment freedoms leads to the recommendation for eliminating all restrictions on adults' access to pornography. Similarly, bolstered by claims of professional expertise and the pro-choice argument, the regulation of abortion is largely managed by the medical profession. In contrast, when their moral rationale seems weaker, reformers tend to recommend tougher forms of regulation. The principled arguments against prohibiting drugs and prostitution, for instance, are not generally seen as compelling, and most reformers advocate relatively complex systems of regulation to, for example, contain the use of decriminalized drugs and minimize the potential problems that might be caused by the drugs' greater availability.

Practicality and principles, then, account for most of the regulators' rhetoric. Sometimes regulation's advocates also acknowledge having vested interests in their plan; proposals to legalize gambling, for instance, usually are designed and promoted by an alliance of the gaming industry (expecting to profit from running gambling) and government officials (anticipating additional tax revenue). Some combination of these three arguments—typically with the emphasis on practicality, rather than morality or interests—forms the basis for most campaigns to regulate illicit marketplaces.

On the other hand, when social control agents regulate an illicit marketplace—usually defining the exchanges as an acceptable, albeit morally tainted activity—criticism often comes from prohibitionists, who are offended by any policy that tolerates behavior they believe should be deviant. In these cases, there is a gap between the officials' moral standards and those of at least an outraged segment of the respectable population. Prohibitionists argue that the regulated marketplace merits harsher social control sanctions, and they may mount moral crusades to push social control agents toward policies of prohibition.

Like regulation's advocates, prohibitionists offer a two-pronged rationale for their proposals. They may raise practical issues, often pointing to atrocities caused by tolerating the marketplace, such as young children being introduced to addicting drugs or viable fetuses being aborted, as evidence of the need to return to prohibition. But they usually prefer to emphasize the moral principles behind prohibition; the contemporary pro-life movement, for example, founds its position on the straightforward argument that abortion is murder. For prohibitionists, principles loom larger than practicality. In this view, arguments regarding the practical benefits of regulation are irrelevant. Evidence that legalized abortion reduces deaths and injuries from botched procedures cannot counterbalance the pro-life movement's claims that abortion is murder. Regulation requires a compromise that the prohibitionists' morality cannot allow.

Thus, whatever policy social control agents adopt toward an illicit marketplace is vulnerable to attack by reformers. Policies of prohibition lead to demands for regulation; policies that regulate the marketplace lead to demands for prohibition. Advocates of regulation and prohibition need not be equally active. Criticism of social control agents may be muted when there is relatively little public concern about an issue or, when there is criticism, it often comes from only one side; those who agree with the current policy's goal usually remain silent, while the policy's opponents tend to speak out. However, on rare occasions, social control agents find themselves sandwiched between vocal critics on each side; the enforcement of marijuana laws in the late 1960s, when officials faced simultaneous demands for stiffer penalties and for decriminalization, is one example.

Whatever the actual level of agitation for reform in a particular illicit marketplace, the potential for attacks on existing policies remains. Regulators and prohibitionists take opposing sides in debates over social control policy, but their concerns parallel one another. Both sometimes have a vested interest in the causes they promote, and both claim that their plans offer practical benefits. But the key similarity between these two breeds of reformers is that both campaigns raise moral issues. Both types of moral crusade challenge the social control agents' moral standards, arguing that the reformers' values are more legitimate. This is a central claim because moral arguments commonly have rhetorical primacy—they are the trump cards—in policy debates.

Reformers of both stripes argue that social control policy translates morality into practice. Morality justifies social control; it serves as the foundation for the entire control apparatus. Therefore, moral arguments potentially carry far more weight than claims about a policy's practicality. When an opponent attacks a particular policy's practical failings, that policy's proponents can safely acknowledge the flaw—if they can simultaneously argue that the policy's moral foundation remains sound. On the other hand, even the most practical, effective policy is vulnerable to attack on moral grounds. Opponents can argue that a string of practical successes cannot justify a policy founded on flawed moral reasoning. This primacy of morality shapes debates over social control policy.

Morality's primacy means that regulators and prohibitionists face very different problems in mounting moral crusades. Regulators' movements are an uphill struggle. It is not enough to show that an existing policy of prohibition is a practical failure. After all, it is rarely possible to completely eradicate deviance. Policies aimed at prohibiting murder and other exploitative crimes cannot keep these predatory acts from occurring, yet this practical failure does not lead to demands for murder's regulation. Although regulators may argue that prohibiting illicit markets is flawed in practice, they must also make a principled case for tolerating the deviant exchanges. These reformers adopt special rhetorical devices to make their case stronger. Thus, they may emphasize the hardships suffered by essentially respectable people who find themselves compelled by circumstances to enter the illicit marketplace; pro-choice advocates, for instance, routinely point to the injustice of laws that might force victims of rape and incest to complete their pregnancies, while marijuana reformers speak of the widespread drug use among the educated middle class and the ruinous effects of a felony arrest on a promising youth's life. A related rhetorical device is to emphasize the size of the illicit market, suggesting that many seemingly respectable people are secret deviants. These techniques help the reformers make a principled case by suggesting that prohibition has evil effects that regulation could alleviate.[24]

In contrast, the primacy of morality makes it much easier for prohibitionists to attack policies of regulation. Vilhelm Aubert's distinction between conflicts of interest (competition) and conflicts of value (dissensus) helps explain the prohibitionists' stance: "One may raise the question whether conflicts of values can be avoided in the same fashion as interest conflicts, e.g., by compromise and mutual resignation relative to what seems the ideal solution. It is no doubt possible to formulate statements that contain some elements from one system of values or description and some from another. . . . The terms of exchange are, however, very uncertain in such dealings. A scent of the illicit often pervades such dealings: 'one cannot trade in values,' 'ideas are not for sale,' 'no bargain with the truth,' etc."[25] Because compromise is hard to achieve, prohibitionists are likely to remain critics of regulatory policies. And because their attacks are likely to emphasize principles, rather than practicality, their rhetoric is usually straightforward. They can simply point to the policy's toleration of deviance, arguing that such compromise threatens the society's moral foundation. Practical concerns—aside from demands that agents receive the resources needed to carry out the prohibitionist reforms—get little attention. While regulators may be willing to compromise on relatively restrictive regulatory policies, prohibitionists normally reject compromise. As a consequence, regulatory policies seem perpetually vulnerable to prohibitionist attacks.

Yet, some regulatory policies do become stable, generally accepted forms of social control. In contemporary America, alcohol and legalized gambling rarely come under serious attack by prohibitionists (although the established toleration of tobacco is currently under assault). Five circumstances seem related to establishing such stable regulatory policies. First, the deviant activity is defined as so widespread as to be uncontrollable through prohibition. Again, the failure of national Prohibition to eradicate drinking is often cited as evidence of the impracticality of prohibitionist policies for large illicit markets. Second, the deviance is defined as a bad habit, a minor vice that need have few serious consequences. In this view, moderate, responsible indulgence appears normal, understandable, and acceptable, although excess—alcoholism, compulsive gambling, and the like—remains deviant. Moderate enjoyment of the bad habit may be linked to approved nonserious activities, such as recreation, entertainment, and sports. This reflects the shift in middle-class values from an emphasis on production to approval of leisure and consumption. Third, a principled rationale based on individual freedom supports the regulatory policy. Thus, no one should be compelled to drink, but neither should the state interfere with those who choose to do so. Fourth, the regulated marketplace often fosters a profitable industry that uses its wealth to further its interests by warding off reformers' campaigns for prohibition. Finally, the deviants are taxed by the regulators, making the policy self-supporting and producing surplus revenues. This gives officials a vested interest in defending regulation from attacks.[26] Under these conditions, regulating deviance can become a taken-for-granted strategy for social control. Otherwise, regulation is likely to remain embattled, attacked on moral grounds.

Lessons from St. Paul

Consider St. Paul's system of de facto regulation of brothel prostitution. The city's policy emerged as a practical response to the problems posed by vice. City officials believed prostitution was inevitable, but they hoped to control the forms it took. They could claim several practical accomplishments: reduced crime and disorder in the brothels; minimal streetwalking; few cases of women being forced into prostitution; and so on. From 1865 to 1883 and beyond, a coalition of practical men—city officials and police officers—protected this system from reformers' attacks.

However, regulation's defenders never established a convincing moral rationale for their policy. The community remained symbolically committed—by the language in its laws—to the prohibition of vice. The system of regulation intentionally twisted those laws, using them to regulate, not prohibit, vice. No one—not the police, not the press, not even the madams—claimed that the laws were misdirected, based on incorrect moral standards. They did not, for example, justify prostitution as a necessary or honorable service, or claim that antivice laws intruded inappropriately into persons' private lives, or make any other principled argument that prohibition was wrong. Regulation's defenders said that prohibition was impractical, not that it was undesirable. In St. Paul, these practical men had the power to implement the system of regulation, but they could not (and did not even try to) change the laws to make regulation an official, formal policy. In St. Louis and other cities, attempts to pass laws officially establishing decriminalized regulatory systems led to angry public debates, and, in every case, prohibitionists using moral arguments fought the new laws and won. Regulation was a widespread policy in the late nineteenth century, but it relied on practicality, rather than morality, for its justification.

What, then, can be learned from St. Paul's experience with regulation? The first, most basic lesson is that social control agents can adopt alternative control strategies. The crude, common-sense distinction between agents committed to prohibition and those who are corrupt is inadequate. Prevention and regulation offer policy alternatives. Moreover, there is room for many subtle policy variations within these general strategies. For instance, consider some alternative approaches to regulation. Gary T. Marx speaks of nonenforcement: "by strategically taking *no enforcement action,* authorities intentionally permit rule breaking." He continues: "In return for noninterference from police (often further bought by the payment of bribes), vice entrepreneurs may agree to engage in self-policing and operate with relative honesty (i.e., run orderly disorderly houses), restrict their activities to one type of vice, stay in a given geographical area, and run low-visibility operations."[27]

The distinction between such informal regulatory practices and St. Paul's system lies in the openness with which the latter operated. St. Paul's police did not ignore the brothels; rather, they announced that they would make monthly arrests. Thus, St. Paul's officials used the existing prohibition apparatus (laws against prostitution, arrest powers, and so on) as a framework for regulation. In turn, such policies can be contrasted with fully legitimized regulatory programs, such as state alcohol control commissions, which feature formal regulatory codes, special enforcement agencies, and the like. Sociologists of social control need to explore the differences among agents' regulatory policies and enforcement mechanisms.

Examining St. Paul's efforts to control vice also reveals the relevance of practicality and morality to debates over regulation. In St. Paul, as elsewhere, regulation emerged from frustration with the practical failures of prohibition. The city's officials believed that prohibition would never eradicate vice, and they sought to adapt to that reality. They agreed to tolerate the presence of prostitution, provided they could regulate the circumstances under which vice operated. The case of St. Paul illustrates the importance of social control agents as advocates of practical, regulatory policies. Social control poses practical problems for agents, and their practical concerns may lead agents to favor regulation as a control strategy. St. Paul's police supported regulation because their principal task was to maintain public order, and regulation gave them a means of minimizing disorder in brothels. In this case, the police were an important group because everyone involved in the debate over vice policy assumed that the police force was the appropriate agency for controlling prostitution. Thus, in addition to their interest in the outcome, the presumed expertise of the police, their knowledge about what could and should be done, let them join the policy debate as a party with some influence. Again, practical concerns—how policies' successes or failures are evaluated and the degree to which those evaluations shape the formation of new social control policies— deserve more attention from sociologists of social control.

Similarly, sociologists must recognize the primacy of morality in policy debates. Too often, their discussions of deviance simplify, and thereby misconstrue, the role of morality in setting social control policy. Functionalist theorists mistakenly assume that norms inevitably reflect an established moral consensus. But conflict theorists are prone to another error: assuming that control policy merely reflects powerful interests and that expressions of morality are mere hypocrisy. Reality is more complex. Policy debates commonly involve groups with competing interests, but they also may involve opponents who are genuinely committed to competing moral principles. The nineteenth-century debates over vice policy in St. Paul and many other cities, like modern disputes about the appropriate ways to control marijuana, abortion, and other deviant exchanges, revolved less around the practical effects of competing policies than around the correct moral posture for society.

The choice of a social control policy, then, belongs in the domain of political scientist Murray Edelman's symbolic politics. The actions of control agents serve as symbolic expressions of the community's moral principles. When these principles are taken for granted, there may be no debate over a policy, regardless of its practical worth. Moral consensus constrains debate:

> Welfare and crime programs that fail also regularly evoke public demands for more of the same policies. In these areas the depiction of public authorities and professionals as effective and benevolent is complemented with the depiction of the poor as pathological. . . . Competent authorities coping with problems caused by the incompetent, sick, or dangerous multitudes who suffer from them is a more vivid perception than an economic system that produces high unemployment levels, low pay, demeaning and stultifying work, and other pathologies. . . . The catalogue of subtle devices through which we authoritatively disseminate and reinforce the conventional beliefs is long. The consequence is that every new alarm about the problems of crime or poverty brings new demands for tougher police measures and more stringent enforcement of the eligibility conditions of welfare legislation.[28]

On the other hand, when moral principles are challenged, alternative social control strategies become visible. And the choice of a strategy, whatever its practical effects, becomes a symbol, representing the dominance of one of the contending moralities. The demise of regulatory vice policies in St. Paul and other cities reveals the importance of these symbols. Reformers refused to accept regulation, not because it did not work but because it required a moral compromise that they found unacceptable.

The vulnerability of St. Paul's regulatory system to repeated moral crusades by prohibitionist reformers offers a final lesson for those who endorse the regulation of illicit marketplaces. During the last thirty years, prohibitionist policies toward illicit markets have come under attack by assorted libertarian and radical reformers advocating regulation or even vindication. Prohibition has been denounced, challenged, and sometimes overturned. Prohibitionist policies toward marijuana and other drugs, gambling, prostitution, pornography, and—perhaps most important—abortion and homosexuality are no longer taken for granted. However, even when these reformers have had success, widespread moral ambivalence remains. People question the morality of tolerating what was once illicit. Prohibitionists play to this ambivalence in their moral crusades against regulation. Vindicating or regulating deviance is not merely a matter of altering social control agents' policies to make them more practical. For the current reforms to remain intact, and for additional reforms to take effect, it will be necessary to fashion and spread a persuasive moral rationale for the new control policies. To be stable, a policy must be seen as right, as well as practical.

Appendix

Principal Brothels in St. Paul, 1865–1883

Firm	Madams	Locations	Period under Madam
1	Henrietta Charles	94 Washington	1865–74
	E. L. Atwood		1874–75
	Maggie Morse		1877–79
	Jennie Bateson		1879–83
2	Mary E. Robinson	20 W. Eighth	1865–74
3	Frank Livingston	Unknown	1865–74
4	Sarah Kimball	Oneida and James	1866–76
	Sarah Kimball	145 Washington	1877–81
	Sarah Kimball	333 Exchange	1882–83
5	Georgia Wright	45 Exchange	1866–72
6	Kate Hutton	7 Hill	1867–75
	Maggie Morse		1875–76
	Kate Hutton		1876–80
	Pauline Bell		1880–83
7	Belle Bowman	1 Jackson	1867–68
	Cora Webber		1868–71
	Lilly Thompson		1872
	Lilly Warren		1872–73
	Kate Bailey		1873–74
	Emma Kaiser		1876

Principal Brothels in St. Paul, 1865–83 (*continued*)

Firm	Madams	Locations	Period under Madam
8	Florence Campbell	93 Eagle	1870–77
	Hattie McBride		1878–81
9	Sarah Mason	56 Jackson	1872–74
10	Lou Adams	14 Washington	1873
	Lou Adams	Cedar and Third	1874
	Lou Adams	11 Nash	1874
11	Hattie McBride	71 Robert	1874–77
12	Addie Fitch	Unknown	1874
13	Amy Leslie	36 E. Fifth	1875–76
	Annie Oleson		1877–80
	Fannie Scheffer		1880–83
14	Mary J. France	82 Cedar	1875–80
	Mary J. France	131 E. Seventh	1881–83
15	Carrie Morrison	92 E. Fifth	1875–82
16	Frankie Brown	72 Eagle	1875–76
	Mattie Gale		1876–80
	Nellie Otis		1880–82
17	Carrie McCarthy	114 E. Fifth	1875–78
	Pauline Bell		1878–80
18	Lizzie Caffrey	66 E. Seventh	1874–78
19	Annie Oleson	137 Jackson	1875–76
20	Clara Morton	42 Eagle	1879–81
21	Kitty Smith	Under the Hill	1880–82
22	Lilla Davis	Unknown	1880–81
23	Emma Lee	Unknown	1880–81
24	Kitty France	Downtown	1880–81
25	Carrie Moore	Under the Hill	1880
26	Ray Lawrence	228 Eagle	1881–83
27	Lou Davis	Unknown	1881–83
28	Alice Percy	387 Sibley	1883

NOTES

The following abbreviations are used for citations to newspapers:

Press	*St. Paul Press*
SPD	*St. Paul Dispatch*
SPDN	*St. Paul Daily News*
SPP	*St. Paul Pioneer*
SPPP	*St. Paul Pioneer Press*
Tribune	*Minneapolis Tribune*

Preface

1. *Press,* August 26, 1871.

2. Kate Millett, *The Prostitution Papers* (New York: Avon, 1973), 17.

3. Examples of popularized histories include Herbert Asbury, *The Barbary Coast* (New York: Knopf, 1933) and *The French Quarter* (New York: Knopf, 1936); Curt Gentry, *The Madams of San Francisco* (Garden City, N.Y.: Doubleday, 1964); and Stephen Longstreet's fictionalized "autobiography," *Nell Kimball: Her Life as an American Madam* (New York: Macmillan, 1970).

4. Recent case studies include Jeffrey S. Adler, "Streetwalkers, Degraded Outcasts, and Good-for-Nothing Huzzies: Women and the Dangerous Class in Antebellum St. Louis," *Journal of Social History* 25 (1991), 737–55;

Jacqueline B. Barnhart, *The Fair but Frail: Prostitution in San Francisco, 1849–1900* (Reno: University of Nevada Press, 1986); George M. Blackburn and Sherman L. Ricards, "The Prostitutes and Gamblers of Virginia City, Nevada: 1870," *Pacific Historical Review* 48 (1979), 239–58; Anne M. Butler, *Daughters of Joy, Sisters of Misery: Prostitutes in the American West, 1865–1890* (Urbana: University of Illinois Press, 1985); Marcia Carlisle, "Disorderly City, Disorderly Women: Prostitution in Ante-Bellum Philadelphia," *Pennsylvania Magazine of History and Biography* 110 (1986), 549–68; Anne P. Diffendal, "Prostitution in Grand Island, Nebraska, 1870–1913," *Heritage of the Great Plains* 16 (1983), 1–9; Timothy J. Gilfoyle, *City of Eros: New York City, Prostitution, and the Commercialization of Sex, 1790–1920* (New York: Norton, 1992); Marion S. Goldman, *Gold Diggers and Silver Miners: Prostitution and Social Life on the Comstock Lode* (Ann Arbor: University of Michigan Press, 1981); Pamela Susan Haag, "'Commerce in Souls': Vice, Virtue, and Women's Wage Work in Baltimore, 1900–1915," *Maryland Historical Magazine* 86 (1991), 292–308; John D. Hewitt and Janet E. Micklish, "Prostitution in Middletown During the Progressive Era," *Wisconsin Sociologist* 24 (1987), 99–111; William L. Hewitt, "Wicked Traffic in Girls: Prostitution and Reform in Sioux City, 1885–1910," *Annals of Iowa* 51 (1991), 123–48; Marilynn Wood Hill, *Their Sisters' Keepers: Prostitution in New York City, 1830–1870* (Berkeley and Los Angeles: University of California Press, 1993); Lucie Cheng Hirata, "Free, Indentured, Enslaved: Chinese Prostitutes in Nineteenth-Century America," *Signs* 5 (1979), 3–29; David C. Humphrey, "Prostitution and Public Policy in Austin, Texas, 1870–1915," *Southwestern Historical Quarterly* 86 (1983), 473–516; Yuji Ichioka, "Ameyuki-san: Japanese Prostitutes in Nineteenth-Century America," *Amerasia* 4 (1977), 1–21; Philip Jenkins, "A Wide-Open City: Prostitution in Progressive Era Lancaster," *Pennsylvania History* (forthcoming); David Kaser, "Nashville's Women of Pleasure in 1860," *Tennessee Historical Quarterly* 23 (1964), 379–82; Carol Leonard and Isidor Wallimann, "Prostitution and Changing Morality in the Frontier Cattle Towns of Kansas," *Kansas History* 2 (1979), 34–53; John S. McCormick, "Red Lights in Zion: Salt Lake City's Stockade, 1908–1911," *Utah Historical Quarterly* 50 (1982), 168–81; Mary Murphy, "The Private Lives of Public Women: Prostitution in Butte, Montana, 1878–1917," *Frontiers* 7 (1984), 30–35; Paula Petrik, *No Step Backward: Women and Family on the Rocky Mountain Mining Frontier, Helena, Montana, 1865–1900* (Helena: Montana Historical Society Press, 1987); Al Rose, *Storyville, New Orleans* (University: University of Alabama Press, 1974); David W. Rose, "Prostitution and the Sporting Life: Aspects of Working Class Culture and Sexuality in Nineteenth Century Wheeling," *Upper Ohio Valley Historical Review* 16 (1987), 7–31; Richard F. Selcer, "Fort Worth and the Fraternity of Strange Women," *Southwestern Historical Quarterly* 96 (1992), 55–86; Neil

Larry Shumsky and Larry M. Springer, "San Francisco's Zone of Prostitution, 1880–1934," *Journal of Historical Geography* 7 (1981), 71–89; Stephen G. Sylvester, "Avenues for Ladies Only: The Soiled Doves of East Grand Forks, 1887–1915," *Minnesota History* 51 (1989), 290–300; Priscilla Wegars, "'Inmates of Body Houses': Prostitution in Moscow, Idaho, 1885–1910," *Idaho Yesterdays* 33 (Spring 1989), 25–37.

5. John C. Burnham, *Bad Habits: Drinking, Smoking, Taking Drugs, Gambling, Sexual Misbehavior, and Swearing in American History* (New York: New York University Press, 1993); David T. Courtwright, *Violent Land: Single Men and Social Disorder from the Frontier to the Inner City* (Cambridge, Mass.: Harvard University Press, 1996); Ned Polsky, *Hustlers, Beats, and Others* (Chicago: Aldine, 1967); Rose, "Prostitution and the Sporting Life"; John C. Schneider, *Detroit and the Problem of Order, 1830–1880* (Lincoln: University of Nebraska Press, 1980).

6. On antibrothel riots, see Michael Feldberg, *The Turbulent Era: Riot and Disorder in Jacksonian America* (New York: Oxford University Press, 1980); Gilfoyle, *City*; Pauline Maier, *From Resistance to Revolution* (New York: Random House, 1972); Schneider, *Detroit*; on social purity, see David J. Pivar, *Purity Crusade: Sexual Morality and Social Control, 1868–1900* (Westport, Conn.: Greenwood, 1973); on the Progressives, see Mark Thomas Connelly, *The Response to Prostitution in the Progressive Era* (Chapel Hill: University of North Carolina Press, 1980); Egal Feldman, "Prostitution, the Alien Woman and the Progressive Imagination, 1910–1915," *American Quarterly* 19 (1967): 192–206; Leslie Fishbein, "Harlot or Heroine: Changing Views of Prostitution, 1870–1920," *Historian* 43 (1980), 23–35; Kay Ann Holmes, "Reflections by Gaslight: Prostitution in Another Age," *Issues in Criminology* 7 (1972), 83–101; Roy Lubove, "The Progressives and the Prostitute," *Historian* 24 (1962), 308–30; Robert E. Riegel, "Changing American Attitudes Toward Prostitution (1800–1920)," *Journal of the History of Ideas* 29 (1968), 437–52; Ruth Rosen, *The Lost Sisterhood: Prostitution in America, 1900–1918* (Baltimore: Johns Hopkins University Press, 1982); Roland Richard Wagner, "Virtue against Vice: A Study of Moral Reformers and Prostitution in the Progressive Era" (Ph.D. diss., University of Wisconsin, 1971); on a modern crusade, see Al Palmquist with John Stone, *The Minnesota Connection* (Van Nuys, Calif.: Bible Voice, 1978).

7. William W. Sanger, *The History of Prostitution* (1858; New York: Arno, 1972); on nineteenth-century regulation, see John C. Burnham, "Medical Inspection of Prostitutes in America in the Nineteenth Century: The St. Louis Experiment and Its Sequel," *Bulletin of the History of Medicine* 45 (1971), 203–18, and "The Social Evil Ordinance: A Social Experiment in Nineteenth Century St. Louis," *Bulletin of the Missouri Historical Society* 27 (1971), 203–17; James B. Jones, "Municipal Vice: The Management of Prostitution in Tennessee's Urban Experience. Part 1: The Experience of

Nashville and Memphis, 1854–1917," and "Part 2: The Examples of Chattanooga and Knoxville, 1838–1917," *Tennessee Historical Quarterly* 50 (1991), 33–41, and 110–22; Rose, *Storyville;* Neil Larry Shumsky, "Tacit Acceptance: Respectable Americans and Segregated Prostitution, 1870–1910," *Journal of Social History* 19 (1986), 665–79; Duane R. Sneddeker, "Regulating Vice: Prostitution and the St. Louis Social Evil Ordinance, 1870–74," *Gateway Heritage* 11 (Fall 1990), 20–47, Howard Brown Woolston, *Prostitution in the United States: Prior to the Entrance of the United States into the World War* (1921; Montclair, N.J.: Patterson Smith, 1969); James L. Wunsch, "Prostitution and Public Policy: From Regulation to Suppression, 1858–1920" (Ph.D. diss., University of Chicago, 1976); on legal brothels in Nevada, see Richard Symanski, "Prostitution in Nevada," *Annals of the Association of American Geographers* 64 (1974), 357–77. Some other countries exhibit more toleration for prostitution, sometimes including formalized systems of regulation. For an overview, see Nanette J. Davis, ed., *Prostitution: An International Handbook on Trends, Problems, and Policies* (Westport, Conn.: Greenwood, 1993).

8. Barbara Meil Hobson, *Uneasy Virtue: The Politics of Prostitution and the American Reform Tradition* (New York: Basic Books, 1987); Jennifer James et al., *The Politics of Prostitution: Resources for Legal Change,* 2nd ed. (Seattle: Social Research Associates, 1977); Valerie Jenness, *Making It Work: The Prostitutes' Rights Movement in Perspective* (Hawthorne, N.Y.: Aldine de Gruyter, 1993); Ronald Weitzer, "Prostitutes' Rights in the United States: The Failure of a Movement," *Sociological Quarterly* 32 (1991), 23–42; Women Endorsing Decriminalization, "Prostitution: A Non-Victim Crime?" *Issues in Criminology* 8 (1973), 137–62.

Chapter 1. Regulating Deviance

1. *SPD,* November 17, 1869; *SPP,* November 17, 18, 1869; *Press,* November 17, 18, 1869.
2. *SPD,* November, 17, 1869; 1870 manuscript census.
3. *SPP,* November, 18, 1869; see also *Press,* November 18, 1869.
4. *SPD,* November 17, 1869.
5. *SPD,* November 17, 1869; May 10–13, 1870; *SPP,* November 18, 1869; January 29, 1870; May 10–13, 1870; *Press,* November 18, 1869; January 29, 1870; May 10–13, 1870.
6. *Press,* November 18, 1869.
7. *SPP,* May 13, 1874; *SPPP,* October 6, 1875; February 14, 1877.
8. *SPP,* November 18, 1869.
9. Milton Rugoff, *Prudery and Passion: Sexuality in Victorian America* (New York: Putnam's, 1971), 347. On the underside of Victorian sexuality, see Peter Cominos, "Late Victorian Sexual Respectability and the Social

System," *International Review of Social History* 8 (1963), 18–48, 216–50; Steven Marcus, *The Other Victorians: A Study of Sexuality and Pornography In Mid-Nineteenth-Century England* (New York: Basic Books, 1966).

10. *SPD*, November 17, 1869.

11. *SPP*, April 28, 1869.

12. There are dozens of sociological discussions of deviance. For an introduction to this literature, see Howard S. Becker, *Outsiders*, rev. ed. (New York: Free Press, 1973); Joel Best and David F. Luckenbill, *Organizing Deviance*, 2nd ed. (Englewood Cliffs, N.J.: Prentice-Hall, 1994); John Lofland, *Deviance and Identity* (Englewood Cliffs, N.J.: Prentice-Hall, 1969).

13. On the classical view of social control, see Morris Janowitz, "Sociological Theory and Social Control," *American Journal of Sociology* 81 (1975), 82–108. On the relevance of this broad definition to deviance, see Allan V. Horwitz, *The Logic of Social Control* (New York: Plenum, 1990); Arthur Lewis Wood, *Deviant Behavior and Control Strategies* (Lexington, Va.: Lexington, 1974). Cross-cultural studies of deviance tend to favor a broad definition, e.g., Edwin M. Lemert, *The Trouble with Evil: Social Control at the Edge of Morality* (Albany: State University of New York Press, 1997). For mainstream, narrower portrayals of social control and deviance, see Kai T. Erikson, *Wayward Puritans* (New York: Wiley, 1966); Edwin M. Schur, *Interpreting Deviance* (New York: Harper and Row, 1979).

14. A clear example of this escalation is the improvements in safe manufacturing and safecracking: Peter Letkemann, *Crime as Work* (Englewood Cliffs, N.J.: Prentice-Hall, 1973), 86–89. On escalation's effects, see Gary T. Marx, "Ironies of Social Control," *Social Problems* 28 (1981), 221–46.

15. Best and Luckenbill, *Organizing Deviance*. Deviant exchanges are included in what Schur calls "victimless crimes": Edwin M. Schur, *Crimes without Victims* (Englewood Cliffs, N.J.: Prentice-Hall, 1965). Schur's critics attack his concept, charging that these offenses have victims, e.g., the drug addict suffers harm, as do the addict's family, people victimized by or frightened of addicts, and so on. The concept of deviant exchange circumvents the issue of who is or is not a victim and emphasizes the sociologically relevant quality of the transaction: participation is voluntary. Some deviant exchanges are trades, in which actors supply each other with reciprocal services, usually a forbidden sexual activity such as homosexuality, sadomasochism, or premarital sex. Other exchanges are sales, in which a customer purchases the good or service from a seller. Deviant sales include prostitution, drug dealing, fencing, and bookmaking. Like respectable trades and sales, these deviant transactions ideally satisfy both participants in the exchange.

16. Vilhelm Aubert and Sheldon Messinger, "The Criminal and the Sick," *Inquiry* 1 (1958), 137–60; Peter Conrad and Joseph W. Schneider, *Deviance and Medicalization*, 2nd ed. (Philadelphia: Temple University Press, 1992).

17. Becker, *Outsiders;* Elliot P. Currie, "Crimes without Criminals," *Law and Society Review* 3 (1968), 7–32; Lofland, *Deviance and Identity;* James Q. Wilson, *Varieties of Police Behavior* (Cambridge: Harvard University Press, 1968).

18. For a review of studies on goal displacement, see Schur, *Interpreting Deviance,* 365–81.

19. Here, as elsewhere, there is a large literature. One of the best studies of tactical issues is Jonathan Rubinstein, *City Police* (New York: Farrar, Straus and Giroux, 1973).

20. Two important exceptions are studies of deviance invention (the process of redefining respectable activities as deviant) and studies of vindication (the process of redefining deviant activities as respectable). Becker, *Outsiders,* 121–63; Joel Best, "Economic Interests and the Vindication of Deviance," *Sociological Quarterly* 20 (1979), 171–82.

Chapter 2. Controlling Brothels in St. Paul

1. Sanger, *History of Prostitution,* 627–28; cf. Connelly, *Response,* 67–90.

2. Pivar, *Purity Crusade;* on the English movement, see Judith R. Walkowitz, *Prostitution and Victorian Society* (New York: Cambridge University Press, 1980). Moralistic images of prostitution also appeared in novels and other popular writing about vice, which consistently depicted the women as wretched and depraved: Connelly, *Response;* Mary de Young, "Help, I'm Being Held Captive! The White Slave Fairy Tale of the Progressive Era," *Journal of American Culture* 6 (1983), 96–99; Laura Hapke, *Girls Who Went Wrong: Prostitutes in American Fiction, 1885–1917* (Bowling Green, Ohio: Bowling Green State University Popular Press, 1989); M. Joan McDermott and Sarah J. Blackstone, "White Slavery Plays in the 1910s," *Theatre History Studies* 16 (1996), 141–56.

3. Rose, *Storyville;* Richard Tansey, "Prostitution and Politics in Antebellum New Orleans," *Southern Studies* 18 (1980), 449–79; Wunsch, "Prostitution and Public Policy." For an argument that respectable people tolerated vice districts because they provided a necessary, visible boundary between morality and immorality, see Shumsky, "Tacit Acceptance."

4. Burnham, "Medical Inspection"; Burnham, "Social Evil Ordinance"; Rose, *Storyville;* Neil Larry Shumsky, "Vice Responds to Reform: San Francisco, 1910–1914," *Journal of Urban History* 7 (1980), 31–47; Sneddeker, "Regulating Vice"; Tansey, "Prostitution and Politics"; Wunsch, "Prostitution and Public Policy."

5. For modern sociological studies, see David J. Bordua, ed., *The Police* (New York: Wiley, 1967); Peter K. Manning, *Police Work* (Cambridge: MIT Press, 1977); William Ker Muir Jr., *Police* (Chicago: University of Chicago Press, 1977); Rubinstein, *City Police;* William B. Sanders, *Detective Work*

(New York: Free Press, 1977); Jerome H. Skolnick, *Justice without Trial* (New York: Wiley, 1966); Wilson, *Varieties of Police.* On nineteenth-century policing, see Eric H. Monkkonen, *Police in Urban America* (New York: Cambridge University Press, 1981).

6. See the sources cited in the preface, n. 4. In general, the relative seclusion of vice in brothels seemed preferable to streetwalking—considered more troubling because it was a form of public disorder associated with the dangerous class: Adler, "Streetwalkers"; Gilfoyle, *City of Eros;* Judith R. Walkowitz, *City of Dreadful Night: Narratives of Sexual Danger in Late-Victorian London* (Chicago: University of Chicago Press, 1992), 21–22. Gilfoyle presents the most ambitious attempt to trace a city's evolving geography of vice. On Oakland, see Lawrence M. Friedman and Robert V. Percival, *The Roots of Justice: Crime and Punishment in Alameda County, California, 1870–1910* (Chapel Hill: University of North Carolina Press, 1981), 94–95.

7. Frank J. Mead and Alix J. Muller, *History of the Police and Fire Departments of the Twin Cities* (Minneapolis: American Land and Title Register Association, 1899), 55.

8. U.S. Census Office, Tenth Census, *Report on the Defective, Dependent, and Delinquent Classes* (Washington, D.C., 1888), 566. For more detailed discussions of crime, vice, and policing in St. Paul, see Joel Best, "Keeping the Peace in St. Paul: Crime, Vice, and Police Work, 1869–74," *Minnesota History* 47 (1981), 240–48; Philip D. Jordan, *Frontier Law and Order* (Lincoln: University of Nebraska Press, 1970), 126–31; and Jordan, *The People's Health: A History of Public Health in Minnesota to 1948* (St. Paul: Minnesota Historical Society, 1953), 243–52.

9. *SPP,* July 14, 1874; city directory, 1869; Chief of Police, "Annual Report," *Proceedings of the Common Council of the City of St. Paul* (St. Paul, 1871), 140; Chief of Police, "Annual Report," *Reports of the City Officers of St. Paul* (St. Paul, 1881), 4–5; Monkkonen, *Police in Urban America,* 59–61.

10. Maurice E. Doran, *History of the St. Paul Police Department* (St. Paul: St. Paul Police Benevolent Association, 1912), 18.

11. Chief of Police, "Annual Report," *Proceedings of the Common Council of the City of St. Paul* (St. Paul, 1875), 209; Doran, *History of the St. Paul Police,* 18.

12. *SPP,* May 22, 1868; October 26, 1873; *SPPP,* March 13, 1879.

13. *SPP,* July 24, 1870; March 10, 1874.

14. *SPPP,* January 21, 1878.

15. *Tribune,* December 23, 1874. The term "inmate" was used generally to refer to prostitutes who worked in brothels; its use here is not intended to carry any special negative connotations.

16. *SPPP,* January 21, 1878. Nineteenth-century estimates for numbers of prostitutes are notoriously inaccurate; reformers' estimates tended to be far

higher than those offered by the authorities: Gilfoyle, *City of Eros,* 57–59;
Hill, *Their Sisters' Keepers,* 26–30.

17. *SPPP,* August 8, 1883.

18. The figures on the number of brothels are based on the forty madams
identified in the appendix. A brothel was presumed to be in operation
throughout the period from the madam's first known arrest to her last
known arrest, unless there was evidence to the contrary. *SPPP,* July 24,
1882.

19. *SPP,* April 28, 1870; June 13, 1872; February 4, 1874; *SPPP,* February 6,
1878; May 14, 1879; June 8, 14, 1881.

20. *SPPP,* August 9, 1883.

21. *SPP,* August 23, 27, 1867; April 22, 1870; *SPPP,* April 7, 1881; June 8,
1881; *Municipal Code of St. Paul,* rev. ed. (St. Paul, 1884), 293–94. The
"roll" used between 1872 and 1874 survives in the back of the manuscript
arrest ledger (hereafter arrest ledger), covering 1869–70 and 1872–74, located in the office of St. Paul's Chief of Police.

22. U.S. Census Office, Tenth Census, *Report on the Defective,* 566–70.
On communities with regulation policies, see Leonard and Wallimann,
"Prostitution and Changing Morality"; Lincoln Steffens, "The Shame of
Minneapolis," *McClure's Magazine* 20 (1903), 229–39; Peggy C. Giordano,
Sandra Kerbel, and Sandra Dudley, "The Economics of Female Criminality:
An Analysis of Police Blotters, 1890–1976" (paper presented to the Society
for the Study of Social Problems, 1978).

23. All but four of the remaining responses were blank; apparently the
census officials viewed no answer and a response of "none" as equivalent.
U.S. Census Office, Eleventh Census, *Report on Crime, Pauperism, and
Benevolence* (Washington, D.C., 1895), 1024–33.

24. George A. Hale, *Police and Prison Cyclopedia,* rev. ed. (Boston:
Richardson, 1893), 194–421.

25. *SPP,* April 15, 1871.

26. Total arrests and fines from annual reports of Chief of Police, 1870
and 1881; vice fines from arrest ledger (1870) and criminal dockets, St. Paul
Municipal Court (Ramsey County Records Center, section 6, shelf 4, vol.
J–M) (1881); Mead and Muller, *History of the Police,* 53.

27. *SPP,* June 13, 1868.

28. *SPP,* September 16, 1869.

29. *SPP,* April 14, 1870; see also *SPPP,* November 16, 1878; June 24, 1880.

30. *SPPP,* March 20, 1882; see also *SPP,* September 2, 1871; July 26, 1872.

31. *SPPP,* February 1, 1881.

32. *SPPP,* June 7, 1880.

33. *SPP,* July 22, 1869; December 2, 1874.

34. *SPP,* March 17, 1868; May 5, 1871; January 3, 1872; February 22, 1874.

35. *SPP*, November 18, 1869; October 13, 1870; *SPPP*, April 1, 1876; March 1, 1880; June 7, 1880.

36. *SPPP*, August 19, 1878; see also *SPP*, July 10, 1867; *SPPP*, March 3, 1882.

37. *SPP*, August 4, 1867; see also June 13, 1866; November 9, 1866; April 26, 1968; December 24, 1868; April 7, 1871; *SPPP*, March 7, 1877; August 8, 1880; April 8, 1881; April 17, 1883.

38. *SPP*, April 21, 1867; April 2, 1870; December 31, 1870; June 18, 1871; March 10–14, 1874; *SPPP*, September 17, 1879.

39. *SPPP*, July 13, 1881; see also November 8, 1878.

40. *SPPP*, February 24, 1880; February 3, 1881.

41. *SPPP*, October 27, 1880.

42. *SPPP*, December 21, 1878.

43. *SPPP*, April 19, 1876; see also July 20, 1875.

44. *SPPP*, June 7, 28, 1879.

45. *SPP*, April 21, 1867; March 11, 1868; *SPPP*, June 8, 1883. On prostitutes resorting to the law, see Hill, *Their Sisters' Keepers*, 145–74.

46. *SPP*, February 6, 1874; see also November 29, 1865; April 8, 1869; January 12, 1871; *SPPP*, August 3, 1876; August 9, 1883.

47. *SPP*, May 1, 1872.

48. *SPPP*, February 7, 1880.

49. In some communities, particularly on the frontier, fines from prostitution composed a substantial portion of total municipal revenue, giving officials a greater economic interest in regulation. Robert A. Harvie and Larry V. Bishop, "Police Reform in Montana, 1890–1918," *Montana* 33 (1983), 46–59; Leonard and Wallimann, "Prostitution and Changing Morality," 40.

Chapter 3. Careers in Brothel Prostitution

1. A. A. E. Taylor, *Seest Thou This Woman?* (Cincinnati: Clarke, 1871), 15.

2. Sanger, *History of Prostitution.*

3. *SPP*, May 13, 1874; *SPPP*, October 6, 1875; February 14, 1877; burial records, Oakland Cemetery, St. Paul.

4. William Acton, *Prostitution* (1870; New York: Praeger, 1968), 72. Frances Finnegan, *Poverty and Prostitution: A Study of Victorian Prostitutes in York* (New York: Cambridge University Press, 1979); Judith R. Walkowitz and Daniel J. Walkowitz, "'We Are Not Beasts of the Field,'" in Mary Hartman and Lois Banner, eds., *Clio's Consciousness Raised* (New York: 1974), 193; Ruth Rosen, "Introduction," in Rosen and Sue Davidson, eds., *The Maimie Papers* (Old Westbury, N.Y.: Feminist Press, 1977), xi–xliv. On the Victorian rhetoric of fallenness, see Amanda Anderson, *Tainted Souls and Painted Faces* (Ithaca, N.Y.: Cornell University Press, 1993); Walkowitz, *City of Dreadful Night.*

5. Becker, *Outsiders*, 24–39.

6. Edward Sagarin, *Deviants and Deviance* (New York: Praeger, 1975), 137–38.

7. Edwin M. Lemert, *Human Deviance, Social Problems, and Social Control* (Englewood Cliffs, N.J.: Prentice-Hall, 1967), 51. For introductions to interactionist studies of deviance and sociological writings about careers, see Earl Rubington and Martin S. Weinberg, eds., *Deviance*, 6th ed. (New York: Allyn and Bacon, 1996); David F. Luckenbill and Joel Best, "Careers in Deviance and Respectability," *Social Problems* 29 (1981), 197–206; Barney G. Glaser, ed., *Organizational Careers* (Chicago: Aldine, 1968).

8. Sources for court records vary over the period: irregular reports of the city justice and the chief of police appeared in *Proceedings of the St. Paul City Council*, 1866–70; the manuscript arrest ledger, 1869–70 and 1872–74; official minutes of the city council, published periodically in the *St. Paul Press*, 1871–72; and the criminal dockets, St. Paul Municipal Court, vol. A–Z, 1875–83. For two gaps in these sources—June 1870 through June 1871, and November 1874 through April 1875—mention of specific arrests in the *St. Paul Pioneer* served to compile a partial record.

9. These different policies produced records of differing detail, particularly in the arrest ledger. On some occasions when both madams and prostitutes were charged, the names of the inmates in each brothel were listed beneath the madam's name, giving a *structured record:*

> Madam 1
> Prostitute 1
> Prostitute 2
> Prostitute 3
> Madam 2
> Prostitute 4
> Prostitute 5
> Prostitute 6
> etc.

On the other months, both categories of names were listed, but the women in each category were grouped together, producing a *categorical record:*

> Madam 1
> Madam 2
> Madam 3
> Prostitute 1
> Prostitute 2
> Prostitute 3
> etc.

But during most months, the prostitutes were not charged individually, and only the madams appeared in *primary records:*

> Madam 1
> Madam 2
> Madam 3
> etc.

Because primary records appear in the vast majority of months under examination, more is known about madams than about their inmates. For a detailed account of one court session where a structured record was produced, see *SPP,* April 22, 1870; for sessions producing primary records, see *SPPP,* April 7, 1881; June 2, 1881; January 3, 1883.

10. Demographic information was drawn from the manuscript census schedules for the federal censuses of 1860, 1870, and 1880, and the state census of 1875, in the cases of nine madams. Three others were described in the register of prostitutes kept at the back of the arrest ledger. Where the women could not be located in either the census schedules or the register, information was taken from the arrests recorded in the ledger proper (for the remaining seven cases). When madams appeared in more than one of these sources, the information frequently differed from one source to the next. In such cases, the census was taken as the most reliable source, with the register second, on the grounds that details about the women were more likely to be recorded accurately on these occasions than in the routine appearances before the police or municipal court.

11. Many of the madams had other arrests, particularly for drunkenness or disorderly conduct. The women's activities were considered newsworthy; newspaper articles mentioned thirty-seven of the forty madams, and some, such as Mary E. Robinson, were the subjects of dozens of stories.

12. Addresses were gathered from St. Paul city directories, 1865–84, the register of prostitutes kept at the back of the arrest ledger, and newspaper articles. Twenty-eight of the madams appeared in city directories during years when they operated brothels (the directories did not list an occupation for most of the women); four madams were located through other sources. The process was complicated by St. Paul's irregular method for numbering houses and by the decision to renumber buildings in the middle of the period studied. *Sanborn's* St. Paul insurance atlases for 1875 and 1885 were used to locate buildings and determine when a house had been renumbered. While the remaining eight madams' precise addresses are not known, at least three operated houses "under the hill," and a fourth was downtown.

13. Arrest ledger; *SPP,* November 7, 1869; March 10-14, 1874; December 2, 1874; *SPPP,* August 24, 1876; November 14, 1877; January 21, 1878; February 4, 1880. For analyses of shifting ownership, management, and

location of New York brothels, see Gilfoyle, *City of Eros;* Hill, *Their Sisters' Keepers,* 100–104, 181-86.

14. Where information about a prostitute appeared in two sources, the rules described in note 10 were followed: census data were considered most reliable, the listing in the arrest ledger's register next, and information recorded under an arrest least accurate. There was one exception: because the arrest ledger's register recorded the woman's age when she first arrived in the city, arrest records were taken as measuring the more typical ages of women working in the brothels.

15. U.S. Census Office, Tenth Census, *Statistics of the Population of the United States,* vol. 1 (Washington, D.C., 1883), 536–37. All forty madams and eighty-nine inmates were apparently white. Occasional newspaper reports mention African-American prostitutes, but never in the context of the established brothels: *SPP,* May 29, 1867; July 23, 1870; *SPP,* July 7, 1877. By 1880, blacks accounted for barely 1 percent of St. Paul's population.

16. A comparison of studies of late-nineteenth- and early-twentieth-century prostitutes reveals some patterns. Generally, prostitutes tended to come from the same places, in roughly the same proportions, as the respectable people in their communities. Chinese and Japanese prostitutes were concentrated in the Far West—a reflection of their control by ethnic criminal syndicates as well as immigration patterns. The women's average age tended to be slightly higher in the West, suggesting that prostitutes could remain active longer where women were in shorter supply. Perhaps some moved west as they grew older and less competitive in the urban marketplace. Most women had lower- or working-class backgrounds. Rosen suggests that, among whites, daughters of immigrants were particularly likely to enter vice, because the immigrant community's ties could not hold the first generation raised in the new land. Cf. San Francisco 1880 manuscript census; Blackburn and Ricards, "Prostitutes and Gamblers"; Craig L. Foster, "Tarnished Angels: Prostitution in Storyville, New Orleans, 1900–1910," *Louisiana History* 31 (1990), 387–97; Goldman, *Gold Diggers;* Hirata, "Free, Indentured, Enslaved"; Ichioka, "Ameyuki-san"; Kaser, "Nashville's Women"; Petrik, *No Step Backward;* Rosen, *Lost Sisterhood,* 137–68; Sanger, *History of Prostitution.*

17. The 1873 city directory counted, by sex, the number of inhabitants in each dwelling. Five brothels appear, with five to thirteen women apiece—figures that would include the madam and any live-in help. Nineteenth-century brothels in other cities averaged four or five inmates. Cf. Fred W. Edmiston, *Washington Slept Here* (New York: Carlton Press, 1977); Goldman, *Gold Diggers;* Rosen, *Lost Sisterhood.*

18. For general discussions of the process of becoming deviant, see Lofland, *Deviance and Identity,* 39–205; David Matza, *Becoming Deviant* (Englewood Cliffs, N.J.: Prentice-Hall, 1969); Rubington and Weinberg, *De-*

viance. Most sociological studies of prostitutes' careers focus on this initial stage: James K. Bryan, "Apprenticeships in Prostitution," *Social Problems* 12 (1965), 287–97; Nanette J. Davis, "The Prostitute: Developing a Deviant Identity," in James M. Henslin, ed., *Studies in the Sociology of Sex* (New York, 1971), 297–322; Paul J. Goldstein, *Prostitution and Drugs* (Lexington, Mass.: Lexington Books, 1979); Diana Gray, "Turning Out: A Study of Teenage Prostitution," *Urban Life and Culture* 1 (1973), 401–25; Barbara S. Heyl, *The Madam as Entrepreneur: Career Management in House Prostitution* (New Brunswick, N.J.: Transaction, 1979); Eleanor M. Miller, *Street Woman* (Philadelphia: Temple University Press, 1986); Mimi H. Silbert and Ayala M. Pines, "Entrance into Prostitution," *Youth and Society* 13 (1982), 471–500.

19. Cf. Cominos, "Late Victorian Sexual Respectability"; Deborah Gorham, "The 'Maiden Tribute of Modern Babylon' Re-examined: Prostitution and the Idea of Childhood in Late Victorian England," *Victorian Studies* 21 (1978), 353–79; McDermott and Blackstone, "White Slavery Plays"; Pivar, *Purity Crusade;* Hartman and Banner, *Clio's Consciousness;* Rosen, *Lost Sisterhood,* 46–50. Organized traffic in women (i.e., white slavery) was limited largely to immigrant communities; women traded their passage for a period of sexual servitude. See Edward J. Bristow, *Prostitution and Prejudice: The Jewish Fight against White Slavery, 1870–1939* (New York: Schocken, 1982); Francesco Cordasco, *The White Slave Trade and the Immigrants* (Detroit: Blaine Ethridge, 1981); Hirata, "Free, Indentured, Enslaved"; Ichioka, "Ameyuki-san."

20. *SPP,* February 25, 1875.

21. *SPPP,* January 28–30, 1879.

22. *SPPP,* January 2–4, 1880.

23. *SPPP,* October 27, 1880.

24. *SPP,* August 19, 1873; *Press,* August 17, 1873.

25. *SPPP,* October 26, 1879.

26. *SPP,* March 4, 1870; *SPPP,* January 26, 1880; May 9, 1882; August 22, 1882.

27. *SPP,* December 31, 1867. Several Progressive Era vice surveys asked women why they entered vice. Ruth Rosen's analysis of these data concludes that white slavery accounted for less than a tenth of new prostitutes. *Lost Sisterhood,* 133.

28. *SPP,* August 30, 1870.

29. *SPP,* November 21, 1871.

30. *SPPP,* November 1, 1878.

31. *SPPP,* October 29, 1875. Cf. Barbara J. Berg, *The Remembered Gate: Origins of American Feminism* (New York: Oxford University Press, 1978), 177–82.

32. U.S. Census Office, Tenth Census, *Report on the Social Statistics of*

Cities, part 2 (Washington, D.C., 1887), 901; *SPPP,* May 18, 1883; June 13, 1883. On occupational choices available to women who became prostitutes, see Hill, *Their Sisters' Keepers,* 63–91; Christine Stansell, *City of Women: Sex and Class in New York, 1789–1860* (New York: Knopf, 1986). On the conditions of domestic servants, see David M. Katzman, *Seven Days a Week* (New York: Oxford University Press, 1978).

33. *SPP,* January 12, 1867.
34. *SPP,* February 15, 1874.
35. *SPP,* January 11, 1871.
36. *SPPP,* April 19, 1876.
37. *SPP,* January 11, 1871.
38. *SPPP,* August 14, 1879; see also *SPP,* August 31, 1867; December 31, 1867; August 12, 1869; January 10, 1871; March 12, 1875; *SPPP,* July 20, 1875; January 30, 1878; April 22, 1878; February 1, 16, 18, 1879; September 20, 1879; September 4, 1881; December 6, 1882.
39. *SPPP,* January 21, 1878.
40. *SPP,* April 20, 1870.
41. *SPP,* August 23, 1872.
42. *SPPP,* May 18, 1882.
43. *SPPP,* January 21, 1881.
44. There are few sociological analyses of the middle stages of deviant careers. For a theoretical statement, see Luckenbill and Best, "Careers in Deviance"; the most detailed case study describes compulsive gamblers: Henry R. Lesieur, *The Chase* (Garden City, N.Y.: Doubleday, 1977). On career shifts among prostitutes, see Goldstein, *Prostitution and Drugs;* Heyl, *Madam;* Jennifer James, "Mobility as an Adaptive Strategy," *Urban Anthropology* 4 (1975), 349–64; Robert Prus and Styllianoss Irini, *Hookers, Rounders and Desk Clerks: The Social Organization of the Hotel Community* (Toronto: Gage, 1980), 50–74.
45. Arrest ledger; *SPP,* September 4, 1867. Migration from one city to another, either by individual choice or through arrangements between madams, was aided by the emergence of vice districts in individual cities and a network of contacts among them. David R. Johnson, "The Origins and Structure of Intercity Criminal Activity, 1840–1920," *Journal of Social History* 15 (1982), 593–605.
46. *SPPP,* December 21, 1878; March 13, 1879; May 4, 1879.
47. *SPPP,* October 22, 1882.
48. *SPP,* August 19, 1873.
49. *Press,* July 19, 22, 1874; August 27, 1874.
50. *SPP,* July 19, 1870; April 15, 1873; February 8, 1874; *Press,* February 12, 1874; August 27, 1874; *SPPP,* April 29, 1875; November 8, 1878; July 25, 1883.
51. *SPP,* April 21, 1867.

52. *SPP*, May 10, 1870.

53. *SPP*, December 31, 1867.

54. *SPPP*, December 12, 1880.

55. *SPP*, May 10, 1870; 1870 manuscript census; city directories for 1868, 1870.

56. Arrest ledger for June–September of 1873 and 1874. The former period had structured records, the latter categorical records. The more formal a city's system of regulation, the easier it is to measure prostitutes' mobility. During the administration of the Social Evil Ordinance in St. Louis, prostitutes had to register and apply for permits to change residences: Sneddeker, "Regulating Vice," 27.

57. Leonard and Wallimann, "Prostitution and Changing Morality"; Petrik, *No Step Backward*; Gentry, *Madams of San Francisco*, 146.

58. Jordan, *Frontier Law*, 131; *SPP*, February 17, 1870; January 12, 1871.

59. *Press*, August 26, 1871.

60. Symanski, "Prostitution in Nevada," 371.

61. During Helena, Montana's early years, opportunities were apparently better; Petrik estimates that one-third of prostitutes were upwardly mobile. Petrik, *No Step Backward*.

62. *SPP*, July 18, 1868.

63. On the process of leaving deviance, see Lofland, *Deviance and Identity*, 209–95; Rubington and Weinberg, *Deviance*, 460–500; Robert A. Stebbins, *Commitment to Deviance* (Westport, Conn.: Greenwood, 1971). There is no sociological study of the process among prostitutes, but see James et al., *Politics of Prostitution*, 44; Prus and Irini, *Hookers, Rounders*, 47–50.

64. *SPP*, November 21–22, 1871.

65. *SPPP*, April 1, 1876.

66. *SPPP*, August 26–27, 1881.

67. *SPPP*, November 9, 1881; see also *SPP*, August 30, 1870; July 28, 1871; *SPPP*, November 13, 1875; April 19, 1879; November 10, 1881; February 9, 1882; January 7, 1883. The newspapers also occasionally reported suicides or suicide attempts by customers who had fallen in love with brothel inmates: *SPP*, April 5, 1872; October 1, 1872; *SPPP*, April 3, 1881.

68. *SPP*, May 10–13, 1870.

69. *SPPP*, February 19, 1882; David T. Courtwright, *Dark Paradise: Opiate Addiction in America before 1940* (Cambridge: Harvard University Press, 1982), 60; Rosen, *Lost Sisterhood*, 98.

70. *SPPP*, November 14, 1877.

71. *SPPP*, April 23, 1878.

72. *SPPP*, May 27, 1874; September 30, 1874; January 24, 1875; October 25, 1875; October 25, 1879; burial records, Oakland Cemetery, St. Paul.

73. Only women who had no arrests on days when brothels were

"pulled" were defined as independent prostitutes, i.e., a woman who was arrested on an odd day in one month but had arrests in later months on days when madams were arrested was assumed to have joined a brothel. Comparison groups are the forty madams and eighty-nine inmates discussed above.

74. *SPP,* April 23, 1870.

75. *SPPP,* August 24, 1876; February 4, 1880; November 10, 1881. For accounts of New York prostitutes with substantial holdings, see Hill, *Their Sisters' Keepers,* 91–106.

76. *SPP,* January 16, 1872. On prospects for marriage, see Hill, *Their Sisters' Keepers,* 281–92.

77. John E. Forliti, "The First Thirty Years of the Home of the Good Shepherd, St. Paul, Minnesota, 1868–1898" (M.A. thesis, St. Paul Seminary, 1962), 52–54; *SPP,* May 27, 1874; *SPPP,* October 29, 1875; October 20, 1877; September 29, 1878; April 1, 1879; October 25, 1879; October 15, 1880. On the high incidence of recidivism among prostitutes who entered institutions of reform, see Hobson, *Uneasy Virtue,* 104–5; Steven Ruggles, "Fallen Women: The Inmates of the Magdalen Society Asylum of Philadelphia, 1836–1908," *Journal of Social History* 16 (1983), 65–82. For an interpretation of houses of refuge as gendered control, see Linda Mahood, *The Magdalenes: Prostitution in the Nineteenth Century* (London: Routledge, 1990).

78. *SPP,* December 19, 1868.

79. *SPPP,* December 21, 1878.

80. *SPPP,* October 15, 1880; see also October 20, 1877.

Chapter 4. The Culture of the Brothel

1. Walkowitz, *Prostitution and Victorian Society,* 25–26.

2. Goldman, *Gold Diggers,* 118.

3. Rosen, *Lost Sisterhood,* 104; cf. Hill, *Their Sisters' Keepers,* 293–319. For a critical review of recent studies, arguing that historians have paid too much attention to reformers, and too little to prostitutes, see Luise White, "Prostitutes, Reformers, and Historians," *Criminal Justice History* 6 (1985), 201–27.

4. *SPP,* August 23, 1872. Cf. Rosen, *The Lost Sisterhood,* 87–91.

5. *SPD,* December 24, 1868.

6. *SPP,* November 11, 1866; August 4, 1867; April 26, 28, 1868; May 2, 1868; July 28, 1871; *SPPP,* February 4, 7, 1880; August 8, 20, 1880; October 16, 1880.

7. *SPPP,* May 16, 1879.

8. *SPP,* November 30, 1865.

9. *SPP,* March 12, 1875; *SPPP,* August 14, 1879; October 24, 26, 1879.

10. *SPPP*, October 4, 1878.

11. *SPP*, May 1, 1867; August 23, 1868; June 15, 1871.

12. *SPP*, November 22, 1871.

13. *SPPP*, November 10, 1881.

14. *SPP*, November 18, 1869.

15. *SPPP*, February 3, 1882; see also *SPP*, October 11, 1868; March 8, 1871; *SPPP*, November 25, 1879.

16. *SPPP*, January 28, 1878.

17. *SPP*, September 16, 1869.

18. *SPPP*, October 19, 1880.

19. *SPP*, August 9, 1868; July 22, 1869; December 2, 1874; *Press*, August 17, 1873; *SPPP*, May 6, 1879; November 24, 1881.

20. *SPP*, April 7, 1871; *SPPP*, November 11, 1875; May 14, 1879; December 12, 1880; April 8, 1881; 1870 manuscript census; 1873 city directory.

21. *SPPP*, January 28, 1878.

22. *SPP*, April 21, 1867; November 21, 22, 1871; *SPPP*, June 13, 1876; August 28, 1879.

23. *SPP*, September 16, 1869.

24. *SPPP*, August 20, 1880; August 27, 1881.

25. *SPPP*, February 15, 1881; August 8, 1881.

26. *SPP*, April 29, 1871; see also April 21, 1867; June 13, 1868. On prostitutes' relationships with men, see Hill, *Their Sisters' Keepers*, 253–80.

27. *SPP*, August 23, 1872; *SPPP*, November 30, 1879.

28. *SPP*, September 1, 1867; August 9, 1872; October 1, 1872; *SPPP*, March 7, 1877; June 4, 1878; November 30, 1879; March 23, 1881; April 8, 9, 1881; April 22, 1883. On the complex relationships between prostitutes and their pimps, see Christina Milner and Richard Milner, *Black Players* (Boston: Little, Brown, 1972); Rosen, *Lost Sisterhood*, 108–10.

29. *SPP*, November 21, 1871; *SPPP*, January 21, 1878; March 1, 1880; January 21, 1881; 1870 manuscript census; 1873 and 1880 city directories.

30. *SPP*, August 11, 1867; *SPPP*, June 3, 1880.

31. *SPP*, November 1, 1873.

32. *SPP*, July 30, 1874.

33. *SPP*, April 22, 1870; 1870 manuscript census.

34. *SPP*, May 2, 1868; Harold Garfinkel, "Conditions of Successful Degradation Ceremonies," *American Journal of Sociology* 61 (1956), 420–24.

35. *SPP*, August 5, 1870.

36. *SPP*, April 22, 1870.

37. *SPP*, May 14, 1868; April 22, 1871.

38. *SPPP*, December 21, 1878.

39. *SPPP*, April 19, 1876.

40. *SPPP*, July 20, 1875; see also *SPP*, June 16, 1870; October 4, 1871; *SPPP*, April 2, 1881; June 2, 8, 1881.

41. *SPPP*, June 14, 1881. On nineteenth-century links between vice and women's fashions, see Gerilyn G. Tandberg, "Sinning for Silk: Dress-for-Success Fashions of the New Orleans Storyville Prostitute," *Women's Studies International Forum* 13 (1990), 229–48; Mariana Valverde, "The Love of Finery: Fashion and the Fallen Woman in Nineteenth-Century Social Discourse," *Victorian Studies* 32 (1989), 168–88.

42. *Municipal Code of St. Paul*, rev. ed. (St. Paul, 1884), 294.

43. *SPP*, August 18, 1868.

44. *SPP*, April 19, 1867; October 11, 1868; March 8, 1871; February 24, 1872; June 20, 1873; *SPPP*, November 25, 1879; February 3, 1882; January 26, 1883. On the links between prostitution and the nineteenth-century theater, see Claudia D. Johnson, "That Guilty Third Tier," *American Quarterly* 27 (1975), 575–84.

45. *SPD*, December 30, 1868.

46. *SPPP*, August 9, 1883.

47. *SPPP*, January 28, 1878.

48. *SPP*, January 29, 1870.

49. *SPP*, December 31, 1867; July 23, 1868; August 9, 1872; *SPPP*, January 21, 1878; December 22, 1878; June 14, 1881.

50. *SPPP*, January 28, 1878. On the role of the seller in deviant sales, see Best and Luckenbill, *Organizing Deviance*.

51. *SPP*, August 19, 1873.

52. *SPP*, May 21, 1867; April 22, 1870.

53. *Press*, August 21, 1873; *SPPP*, December 21, 1878.

54. *SPP*, November 18, 1869; May 10–11, 1870.

55. *SPP*, May 21, 1867; July 23, 1868; August 5, 1870; September 18, 1870; July 22, 1871; January 3, 1872; *SPPP*, December 9, 1878; June 24, 1880; June 3, 1882.

56. *SPP*, May 27, 1869.

57. *SPP*, December 2, 1874.

58. *SPP*, November 29, 1865; April 8, 1869; *SPPP*, August 3, 1876.

59. *SPP*, February 17, 1870; January 22, 1871.

60. *SPPP*, July 7, 1877; see also October 8, 1881; January 19, 1883.

61. *SPP*, September 4, 1867.

62. Arrest ledger; *SPP*, September 10, 1867; April 22, 1870; *SPPP*, February 1, 1881. There is remarkably little firsthand information about customers, but see the notorious English sexual autobiography, Anonymous, *My Secret Life* (1894; New York: Grove Press, 1966), as well as the oral history transcripts in Rose, *Storyville*, 153–63. For a modern sociological discussion, see Harold R. Holzman and Sharon Pines, "Buying Sex: The Phenomenology of Being a John," *Deviant Behavior* 4 (1982), 89–116.

63. *SPPP*, January 25, 1878.

64. *SPPP*, July 23, 1881.

65. *SPPP*, July 23, 1881; Rose, *Storyville;* Tansey, "Prostitution and Politics"; Wegars, "'Inmates of Body Houses,'" 27–29; Wunsch, "Prostitution and Public Policy." For an analysis of landlords in contemporary American prostitution, see Gail Sheehy, *Hustling: Prostitution in Our Wide-Open Society* (New York: Delacorte, 1971).

66. *SPDN*, January 9, 1933.

67. *SPPP*, June 8, 11, 1883; August 8, 1883. For a detailed discussion of modern prostitution's symbiotic relationship with bars and hotels, see Prus and Irini, *Hookers, Rounders.* On the emergence of the vice district as a nineteenth-century urban scene, see Johnson, "Origins and Structure."

68. *SPDN*, January 9, 1933.

69. *Press*, August 26, 1871.

70. David R. Johnson, *Policing the Urban Underworld: The Impact of Crime on the Development of American Police* (Philadelphia: Temple University Press, 1979), 145-81; Rose, *Storyville*, 42–47; Lloyd Wendt and Herman Rogan, *Bosses in Lusty Chicago* (1943; Bloomington: Indiana University Press, 1967). This paragraph, like most historical accounts of American prostitution during this period, is most applicable to brothels. Streetwalking and other forms of prostitution are less accessible to study. In the new social history, as in the old, the upper reaches, even of the underworld, are more easily examined. Moreover, there were some important ethnic differences in the organization of vice: black prostitution more often involved streetwalking; Asian criminal syndicates often purchased women in China or Japan and imported them, forcing them to serve terms of sexual slavery in West Coast Chinatown brothels; organized procuring (i.e., white slavery) also served as a means of immigration for some Jewish and other European women. Bristow, *Prostitution and Prejudice;* Cordasco, *White Slave Trade;* Hirata, "Free, Indentured, Enslaved"; Ichioka, "Ameyuki-san"; Ivan Light, "The Ethnic Vice Industry, 1880–1944," *American Sociological Review* 42 (1977), 464–79.

Chapter 5. Respectable Responses to Regulation

1. *SPP*, February 16, 1867; see also *Tribune*, December 23, 1874; *Press*, December 23, 1874.

2. On synonyms for prostitute in nineteenth-century Virginia City, see Goldman, *Gold Diggers*, 58–59.

3. *SPP*, May 10–13, 1870; March 19–22, 1872.

4. *SPD*, December 24, 29, 30, 1868; *SPP*, December 25, 30, 31, 1868. On St. Paul's press during this period, see Richard B. Side, "The Influence of Editorship and Other Forces on the Growth of the *St. Paul Pioneer-Press*, 1849-1909" (Ph.D. diss., University of Missouri, 1939), 65-70.

5. *SPP*, April 29, 1869.

6. *SPPP*, October 22, 1878.

7. *Press*, August 17, 1873.

8. *SPP*, August 19, 21, 1873.

9. *SPPP*, March 12, 1878.

10. *SPPP*, October 1, 1878; June 10, 1880; April 8, 1881.

11. *SPP*, December 6, 1865; May 2, 1868; July 27, 1871; March 11, 13, 1874; *SPPP*, December 3, 1879; November 27, 30, 1881; December 1, 2, 1881; July 26, 1883. On the reluctance of nineteenth-century juries to convict defendants, see Roger Lane, *Violent Death in the City* (Cambridge: Harvard University Press, 1979), 66–70.

12. *SPPP*, February 24, 1880.

13. *SPP*, June 17, 18, 1871.

14. *SPPP*, March 29, 1876.

15. *SPP*, November 30, 1865; *SPPP*, October 29, 1875; March 23, 25, 1876.

16. *SPP*, November 30, 1865.

17. *SPPP*, October 29, 1875.

18. *SPPP*, March 23, 1876.

19. *SPP*, April 23, 1870.

20. *SPPP*, October 29, 1875; see also January 11, 15, 1878; June 13, 1881; December 19, 1881.

21. *SPPP*, October 29, 1875.

22. *SPP*, November 30, 1865.

23. *SPPP*, March 25, 1876.

24. *SPPP*, July 31, 1879.

25. *SPPP*, December 19, 1881.

26. On moral crusades, see Becker, *Outsiders*, 147–63.

27. *SPP*, April 22, 1870.

28. *SPP*, April 22, 1870; *SPD*, April 22, 1870.

29. *SPP*, July 28, 1870; see also June 16, 1870; July 29–30, 1870; *SPD*, July 27–28, 1870.

30. *SPP*, February 4, 1874.

31. *SPP*, February 4, 1874; see also *Press*, February 4, 1874.

32. *SPP*, February 10, 12, 17, 1874; May 13, 1874.

33. *Press*, February 24, 1874; see also *SPP*, February 6, 8, 1874.

34. *SPP*, March 11–14, 1874.

35. *Press*, March 20, 1874.

36. *Press*, June 18, 1874; arrest ledger (1874).

37. *SPPP*, January 11, 1878.

38. *SPPP*, January 15, 21, 22, 25, 28, 1878; February 6, 1878.

39. *SPPP*, March 6, 1878; see also February 6, 15, 18-19, 1878; March 9, 1878.

40. *SPPP*, March 6, 1878.

41. *SPPP*, April 17, 1878; June 5, 1878.

42. *SPPP*, March 10, 1878.

43. *SPPP*, April 23, 1878; criminal dockets, St. Paul Municipal Court, vol. E–G (1878).

44. *SPPP*, May 15, 1879; see also May 14, 16–17, 1879.

45. *SPPP*, May 20, 1879; see also May 18, 1879.

46. *SPPP*, June 21, 1879; October 12, 14, 1879.

47. *State v. Oleson* (June 9, 1880), *Minnesota Reports* 26, 507–21. Henrietta Charles had advanced a similar argument and lost in an earlier case: *State v. Charles* (1870–71), *Minnesota Reports* 16, 426–34.

48. *SPPP*, June 27, 1880; see also June 10, 1880.

49. *SPPP*, July 9, 1880.

50. *SPPP*, June 8, 13, 1881.

51. *SPPP*, July 23, 24, 28, 1881; October 11–14, 1881.

52. *SPPP*, November 26, 27, 30, 1881; December 1, 1881.

53. *SPPP*, October 14, 1881.

54. *SPPP*, December 2, 1881.

55. *SPPP*, May 26, 1882; October 22, 1882; November 26, 1882; January 3, 1883; *State v. Lee* (October 21, 1882), *Minnesota Reports* 29, 445–62.

56. *SPPP*, July 25, 1883; see also May 1, 2, 1883; June 3, 8, 9, 11, 29, 1883; July 21, 26, 1883; August 8, 1883.

57. *SPPP*, July 26, 1883.

58. *SPPP*, August 8, 1883; see also June 8, 11, 1883.

59. *SPPP*, August 9, 1883.

60. His unpopular vice policy accounted for O'Brien's decision not to seek reelection. Nearly thirty years later, a St. Paul physician recalled: "Not long ago a mayor killed himself politically here by enforcing the laws he found on the statute books regarding this evil. After his single term the agitation died down. Suppression would be opposed by those deriving income from the business. The unknown property owner, the dealers in supplies to these places, perhaps brewers or who not. Possibly rich men might aid the opposition." Charles E. Smith Jr., "Some Observations on Public Health and Morality," *St. Paul Medical Journal* 14 (1912), 199–200. Cf. Thomas D. O'Brien, *There Were Four of Us or, Was It Five* (St. Paul, 1936). *SPDN*, January 10, 1933.

61. *SPPP*, May 5, 1885.

62. *SPPP*, May 6, 1885. Election districts were given in *Municipal Code of St. Paul*, rev. ed. (St. Paul, 1884), 297–303. District boundaries were compared with the brothel locations described in chapter 2. Five districts contained established brothels: the first districts of the first, second, third, and fourth wards, and the third ward's second district.

63. *SPPP*, June 3, 1885.

64. *SPPP*, September 2, 1885.

65. Doran, *History of St. Paul Police*, 29; Mead and Muller, *History of*

the Police, 62; criminal dockets, St. Paul Municipal Court, vol. EE–GG (1885).

Chapter 6: *Officials and the Decline of Regulation*

1. Prostitutes (and alleged prostitutes) did not always fare so well under regulation. In nineteenth-century England and France, regulatory programs that included compulsory medical inspections met considerable resistance from women who found the programs oppressive. Judy Coffin, "Artisans of the Sidewalk," *Radical History Review* 26 (1982), 89–101; Walkowitz, *Prostitution and Victorian Society.*

2. *SPPP*, February 6, 1878.

3. *SPPP*, May 14, 1879; see also *SPD*, July 27, 1870; *SPP*, July 28, 1870; February 4, 1874; *Press*, February 4, 1874; *SPPP*, June 8, 1881; June 3, 1885.

4. *SPP*, July 30, 1870.

5. An 1890 handbook for St. Paul's police officers details the department's rules for arrest that provided the basis for these constraints:

> 9. Arrests for misdeameanor can never be made upon information. To justify them the officer must either have a warrant or see the act committed. . . .

> 12. In all cases under city ordinances, warrants should be taken out before arrest, unless the party to be arrested is engaged in actual violence, or some other conduct in the officer's presence, which it is necessary to stop at once.

Manual of the Police Force of the City of St. Paul, State of Minnesota, Adopted by Robert A. Smith, Mayor, and John Clark, Chief of Police (St. Paul: Pioneer Press, 1890), 47–48. *SPP*, April 22, 1870; July 28, 1870; *SPPP*, March 6, 10, 1878; May 14, 1879; July 23, 1881.

6. *SPP*, April 22, 1870.

7. *SPPP*, May 5, 1885.

8. *SPDN*, January 10, 1933. The disposition of fines from regulating vice varied among cities: in Grand Island, "All revenues were deposited in the city's school fund"; in Chattanooga, critics complained that police brought cases (and revenues) to state, rather than municipal courts; while the East Grand Forks city treasury received much less than the total levied because someone "siphoned off" the difference: Diffendal, "Prostitution in Grand Island," 2; Jones, "Municipal Vice, Part 2," 110; Sylvester, "Avenues for Ladies Only," 298.

9. *SPP*, June 9, 1870; August 17, 1872; January 16–17, 1873; March 23, 1873; March 7, 1874; August 2, 1874; *SPPP*, November 24, 1878; April 26,

1879; May 15, 1879; July 24, 1879; January 27, 1881; August 9, 1883; *SPDN*, January 9, 10, 13, 1933.

10. Arrest ledger. On the social organization of nineteenth-century gambling, see David R. Johnson, "A Sinful Business: The Origins of Gambling Syndicates in the United States," in David R. Bayley, ed., *Police and Society* (Beverly Hills, Calif.: Sage, 1977), 17–47.

11. Chief of Police, "Annual Report," *Proceedings of the Common Council of the City of St. Paul* (St. Paul, 1891 and 1911).

12. Best, "Keeping the Peace"; Chief of Police, "Annual Report," *Proceedings of the Common Council of the City of St. Paul* (St. Paul, 1891 and 1911).

13. Ann Regan, "The Irish," in June D. Holmquist, ed., *They Chose Minnesota* (St. Paul: Minnesota Historical Society Press, 1981), 130–52; *SPDN* January 9–February 2, 1933; Chief of Police, "Annual Report," *Proceedings of the Common Council of the City of St. Paul* (St. Paul, 1890–1914).

14. Doran, *History of St. Paul Police,* 45.

15. Jordan, *People's Health,* 251.

16. Doran, *History of St. Paul Police,* 54, 82.

17. Jordan, *People's Health,* 251.

18. Steffens, "Shame of Minneapolis."

19. Board of Police Commission, *Minneapolis City Officers' Annual Reports* (Minneapolis, 1903).

20. Board of Police Commission, *Minneapolis City Officers' Annual Reports* (Minneapolis, 1904), 497.

21. *Report of the Vice Commission of Minneapolis* (Minneapolis: Hall, 1911), 71.

22. Berg, *Remembered Gate,* 176–222; Pivar, *Purity Crusade.*

23. Connelly, *Response,* 6–7; Peter Baldwin, "Antiprostitution Reform and the Use of Public Space in Hartford, Connecticut, 1878–1914," *Journal of Urban History* 23 (1997), 709–38; Kathleen Daly, "The Social Control of Sexuality: A Case Study of the Criminalization of Prostitution in the Progressive Era," *Research in Law, Deviance and Social Control* 9 (1988), 171–206; Feldman, "Prostitution, the Alien Woman"; Fishbein, "Harlot or Heroine?"; Hobson, *Uneasy Virtue;* Holmes, "Reflections by Gaslight"; David J. Langum, *Crossing the Line: Legislating Morality and the Mann Act* (Chicago: University of Chicago Press, 1994); Lubove, "Progressives and the Prostitute"; Riegel, "Changing American Attitudes"; Rosen, *Lost Sisterhood;* Wagner, "Virtue against Vice."

24. Connelly, *Response,* 136–50. For case studies of war-related campaigns against prostitution, see Garna L. Christian, "Newton Baker's War on El Paso Vice," *Red River Valley Historical Review* 5 (1980), 55–67; Richard A. Greer, "Collarbone and the Social Evil," *Hawaiian Journal of History* 7 (1973), 3–17; James R. McGovern, "Sporting Life on the Line,"

Florida Historical Quarterly 54 (1975), 131–44; Elizabeth C. MacPhail, "When the Red Lights Went Out in San Diego," *Journal of San Diego History* 20 (1974), 1–28; David J. Pivar, "Cleansing the Nation: The War on Prostitution, 1917–21," *Prologue* 12 (1980), 29–40; Rose, *Storyville*, 166–81; James A. Sandos, "Prostitution and Drugs: The United States Army on the Mexican-American Border, 1916–1917," *Pacific Historical Review* 49 (1980), 621–45.

25. John C. Burnham, "The Progressive Era Revolution in American Attitudes toward Sex," *Journal of American History* 59 (1973), 885–908.

26. The Progressives' antivice campaign in New York initially claimed prohibition was at hand; for an optimistic assessment, see George J. Kneeland, *Commercialized Prostitution in New York City*, 4th ed. (1917; Montclair, N.J.: Patterson Smith, 1969); see also Gilfoyle, *City of Eros*, 306–14. On Luciano, see Alan Block, *East Side—West Side: Organizing Crime in New York, 1930–1950* (Cardiff: University College Cardiff Press, 1980), 141–47.

27. On the extortionate organization of illicit markets, see Joel Best, "Crime as Strategic Interaction: The Social Organization of Extortion," *Urban Life* 11 (1982), 107–28; Thomas C. Schelling, "What Is the Business of Organized Crime?" *American Scholar* 40 (1971), 643–52. For an argument that illicit markets rarely become centralized, see Peter Reuter, *Disorganized Crime* (Cambridge: MIT Press, 1983).

28. Shumsky and Springer, "San Francisco's Zone," 83. On San Francisco, see Ivan Light, "From Vice District to Tourist Attraction: The Moral Career of American Chinatowns, 1880–1940," *Pacific Historical Review* 43 (1974), 367–94; Humbert S. Nelli, *The Business of Crime: Italians and Syndicated Crime in the United States* (New York: Oxford University Press, 1976), 184–87. Sally Stanford's autobiography describes an independent San Francisco brothel, *The Lady of the House* (New York: Putnam's, 1966).

29. On Chicago, see John Landesco, *Organized Crime in Chicago* (1929; Chicago: University of Chicago Press, 1968), 25–43; Walter C. Reckless, *Vice in Chicago* (Chicago: University of Chicago Press, 1933).

30. On the decline of the modern brothel, see Heyl, *Madam as Entrepreneur*.

31. Ivan Light, "Ethnic Vice Industry"; Polsky, *Hustlers, Beats*, 31–37; Edward Shorter, *The Making of the Modern Family* (New York: Basic Books, 1975), 245–54.

32. For studies of vice enforcement during the 1960s, see Pamela A. Roby, "Politics and Criminal Law: Revision of the New York State Penal Law on Prostitution," *Social Problems* 17 (1969), 83–109; Skolnick, *Justice without Trial*, 96–111; Wilson, *Varieties of Police*, 99–110.

33. Edwin M. Schur, *The Politics of Deviance* (Englewood Cliffs, N.J.: Prentice-Hall, 1980), 204–7.

34. Barbara Heyl, "Prostitution: An Extreme Case of Sex Stratification," in Freda Adler and Rita James Simon, eds., *The Criminology of Deviant Women* (Boston: Houghton Mifflin, 1979), 196; see also Freda Adler, *Sisters in Crime: The Rise of the New Female Criminal* (New York: McGraw-Hill, 1975), 55–83; Kathleen Barry, *Female Sexual Slavery* (Englewood Cliffs, N.J.: Prentice-Hall, 1979); Jennifer James et al., *Politics*; Millett, *Prostitution Papers*; Sheehy, *Hustling*; Women Endorsing Decriminalization, "Prostitution."

35. Hobson, *Uneasy Virtue*; James et al., *Politics*; Jenness, *Making It Work*.

Chapter 7. Social Control: Strategy, Practicality, and Morality

1. Marx, "Ironies of Social Control," 222.

2. The typology of control strategies offered below makes no claim of completeness. For alternative typologies of control styles or systems, see Donald Black, *The Behavior of Law* (New York: Academic Press, 1976), 4–6; Horwitz, *Logic of Social Control*; Wood, *Deviant Behavior*, 51–59.

3. Jack P. Gibbs, *Crime, Punishment, and Deterrence* (New York: Elsevier, 1975).

4. Best and Luckenbill, *Organizing Deviance*; Donald Black, *The Manners and Customs of the Police* (New York: Academic Press, 1980); Albert J. Reiss, *The Police and the Public* (Cambridge: MIT Press, 1971).

5. John I. Kitsuse and Aaron V. Cicourel, "A Note on the Uses of Official Statistics," *Social Problems* 11 (1963), 131–39.

6. Michael Tonry and David P. Farington, eds., *Building a Safer Society: Strategic Approaches to Crime Prevention*, vol. 19 of *Crime and Justice* (Chicago: University of Chicago Press, 1995); Charles Murray, "The Physical Environment," in James Q. Wilson and Joan Petersilia, eds., *Crime* (San Francisco: Institute for Contemporary Studies, 1995), 349–61.

7. On inducement, see James Q. Wilson, *Thinking about Crime*, rev. ed. (New York: Basic Books, 1983). Of course, advocates of prohibition argue that that policy's deterrent effects represent the most effective way to discourage deviant motives.

8. On such quasi-experimental designs, see Donald T. Campbell and H. Laurence Ross, "The Connecticut Crackdown on Speeding," *Law and Society Review* 3 (1968), 33–53.

9. On contemporary alcohol regulation, see Patricia A. Adler and Peter Adler, "Dry with a Wink: Normative Clash and Social Order," *Urban Life* 12 (1983), 123–39; Joseph R. Gusfield, *Contested Meanings: The Construction of Alcohol Problems* (Madison: University of Wisconsin Press, 1996).

10. Best and Luckenbill, *Organizing Deviance*; Herbert L. Packer, *The*

Limits of the Criminal Sanction (Stanford: Stanford University Press, 1968); Schur, *Crimes without Victims.*

11. Burnham, *Bad Habits.*

12. David Piers, "Eighteenth Century Gaming," in James A. Inciardi and Charles E. Faupel, eds., *History and Crime* (Beverly Hills, Calif.: Sage, 1980), 169–92.

13. Ronald A. Farrell and Carol Case, *The Black Book and the Mob: The Untold Story of the Control of Nevada's Casinos* (Madison: University of Wisconsin Press, 1995); John F. Galliher and John R. Cross, *Morals Legislation without Morality: The Case of Nevada* (New Brunswick, N.J.: Rutgers University Press, 1983); Jerome H. Skolnick, *House of Cards: The Legalization and Control of Casino Gambling* (Boston: Little, Brown, 1978).

14. Best, "Economic Interests"; Galliher and Cross, *Morals Legislation;* Skolnick, *House of Cards.*

15. For examples of these problems, see Eva Bertram et al., *Drug War Politics* (Berkeley and Los Angeles: University of California Press, 1996); Alfred R. Lindesmith, *The Addict and the Law* (New York: Vintage, 1965); Marx, "Ironies of Social Control"; Rubinstein, *City Police;* Skolnick, *Justice without Trial.*

16. The successful eradication of the illicit traffic in ether in late-nineteenth-century Ulster illustrates some of these factors. Ether was a popular intoxicant because it was cheaper than alcohol. After the authorities began to enforce the laws against ether, the traffic stopped. There were no local manufacturers, and ether was too bulky to smuggle easily. Enforcement drove the cost of ether up so that would-be suppliers could no longer compete against alcohol. K. H. Connell, *Irish Peasant Society* (Oxford, Eng.: Clarendon Press, 1968), 87–108.

17. On the Temperance movement, see Joseph R. Gusfield, *Symbolic Crusade* (Urbana: University of Illinois Press, 1963). On the need for substitute satisfactions, see Jay Livingston, *Compulsive Gamblers: Observations on Action and Abstinence* (New York: Harper and Row, 1974).

18. Several recent analyses, grounded in case studies, extend the theory of illicit markets and challenge the claim that these markets are ordinarily vulnerable to monopoly control, i.e., control by organized crime. Specific structural conditions, such as the involvement of a single, corrupt social control agency, seem necessary for centralized control to emerge. Otherwise, the market will feature competition among entrepreneurial suppliers. Patricia A. Adler, *Wheeling and Dealing* (New York: Columbia University Press, 1985); Mark Harrison Moore, *Buy and Bust: The Effective Regulation of an Illicit Market in Heroin* (Lexington, Mass.: Lexington, 1977); Reuter, *Disorganized Crime.*

19. The campaign to decriminalize marijuana offers the best example: Becker, *Outsiders,* 135–46; Erich Goode, *The Marijuana Smokers* (New

York: Basic Books, 1970); John Kaplan, *Marijuana: The New Prohibition* (New York: World, 1970).

20. Richard Quinney, *Class, State, and Crime: On the Theory and Practice of Criminal Justice* (New York: McKay, 1977), 45. Steven Spitzer argues that an overproduction of deviants may lead to campaigns to normalize (i.e., regulate) deviance: "Toward a Marxian Theory of Deviance," *Social Problems* 22 (1975), 638–51. See also Best, "Economic Interests"; Burnham, *Bad Habits*; Donald T. Dickson, "Bureaucracy and Morality: An Organizational Perspective on a Moral Crusade," *Social Problems* 16 (1968), 143–56; Gusfield, *Symbolic Crusade.* On contemporary moral debates, see Peter Skerry, "The Class Conflict over Abortion," *Public Interest* 52 (1978), 69–84; Louis A. Zurcher Jr. and R. George Kirkpatrick, *Citizens for Decency: Antipornography Crusades as Status Defense* (Austin: University of Texas Press, 1976); Galliher and Cross, *Morals Legislation*; John F. Galliher and Linda Basilick, "Utah's Liberal Drug Laws: Structural Foundations and Triggering Events," *Social Problems* 26 (1979), 284–97.

21. Erikson, *Wayward Puritans*; Garfinkel, "Conditions."

22. On public perceptions of crime seriousness, see Peter H. Rossi et al., "The Seriousness of Crimes," *American Sociological Review* 39 (1974), 224–37. On folk crimes, see H. Laurence Ross, "Traffic Law Violation," *Social Problems* 8 (1961), 231–41; Michele Wilson, "Folk Crime," *Deviant Behavior* 4 (1983), 123–40.

23. Jenness, *Making It Work*; U.S. Commission on Obscenity and Pornography, *Report* (Washington, D.C.: U.S. Government Printing Office, 1970).

24. For a related discussion of reformers' purposes and rhetoric, see Joel Best, *Threatened Children: Rhetoric and Concern about Child-Victims* (Chicago: University of Chicago Press, 1990); Malcolm Spector and John I. Kitsuse, *Constructing Social Problems* (Menlo Park, Calif.: Cummings, 1977).

25. Vilhelm Aubert, *The Hidden Society* (Totowa, N.J.: Bedminster Press, 1965), 90.

26. Burnham, *Bad Habits*; Ronald J. Troyer and Gerald E. Markle, *Cigarettes* (New Brunswick, N.J.: Rutgers University Press, 1983); Skolnick, *House of Cards.* A similar phenomenon may be found in legalized abortion; the profits from these procedures give the medical profession a vested economic interest in defending abortion's availability.

27. Marx, "Ironies of Social Control," 222, 229.

28. Murray Edelman, *Political Language: Words That Succeed and Policies That Fail* (New York: Academic Press, 1977), 149; see also Edelman, *The Symbolic Uses of Politics* (Urbana: University of Illinois Press, 1964); Edelman, *Constructing the Political Spectacle* (Chicago: University of Chicago Press, 1988).

INDEX

The History of Crime and Criminal Justice Series

David R. Johnson and Jeffrey S. Adler, Series Editors

The series explores the history of crime and criminality, violence, criminal justice, and legal systems without restrictions as to chronological scope, geographical focus, or methodological approach.

Murder in America
A History
Roger Lane

Race, Labor, and Punishment in the New South
Martha A. Myers

Men and Violence
Gender, Honor, and Rituals in Modern Europe and America
Edited by Pieter Spierenburg